BEYOND *the* BROAD PATH

Embracing the Narrow Way *of* Certainty in Christ

JOHN STEPHEN FREY

LUCIDBOOKS

Beyond the Broad Path: Embracing the Narrow Way of Certainty in Christ

Published by Lucid Books in Houston, TX
www.LucidBooks.com

ISBN: 978-1-63296-992-7 (Paperback)
ISBN: 978-1-63296-993-4 (Hardback)
eISBN: 978-1-63296-994-1

Special Sales: Most Lucid Books titles are available in special quantity discounts. Custom imprinting or excerpting can also be done to fit special needs. Contact Lucid Books at Info@LucidBooks.com

CONTENTS

FOREWORD

In a world that's confusing, loud and full of conflicting signals, finding a clear path forward might seem impossible. Perhaps you're tired of searching. Tired of the noise and racket surrounding you. You're seeking an answer that is real, lasting—and deeply true. If that's you, this book is an invitation to pause, take a deep breath, and begin your journey toward enduring hope and clarity.

And a vibrant faith in Jesus Christ.

John didn't write a textbook. He wrote a shared map. He has given us a GPS—if you will. And I trust it will help you chart a course from doubt and searching to the author of conviction and truth. Within these pages, John will help you secure an honest reflection on the universal questions that ultimately lead to the cross.

The foot of the cross . . .

But the journey doesn't end with belief. It starts there. If you already know Christ, this book will serve as a challenge and potent call to action.

We're living epistles, and those around us desperately

need to see and experience the genuine and transformative love of God. It should be reflected in our everyday lives. I trust John's writing will serve as a fresh wind of encouragement. And I pray it will stir your soul to truly *reflect Christ in all things*. Your work, words, and relationships with those who follow Christ—as well those who don't know Him—should reflect Christ's love.

Whether you're seeking the truth found in Christ for the first time or you're striving to live His love out on a daily basis, John's words will help you find what you're looking for—the truth of the gospel.

Think of it this way. This book was written for you. God ordained it. So, dive in. And may your life make a difference to those around you.

You, my friend, are in for a *spiritual treat*. So, grab your coffee or tea and settle into that comfortable chair. And enjoy the journey!

—Jill Taylor
January 2026
Founder and Host of *Choose Life Radio*
www.chooseliferadio.com

Introduction:

THE CROSSROADS

The journey of faith is often described as a race, a battle, or a constant walk. We all start with fervor, yet somewhere along the way, the fire can dim, leaving us feeling disconnected or adrift. If you identify as a believer in Jesus Christ, I must ask: Have you allowed your faith to become stagnant or lukewarm? Has the daily grind replaced the vibrant connection you once knew? If a shadow of guilt, failure, or exhaustion is holding you back, hear this truth today: Your race is not over. Now is the moment to leave the weight of past regrets and perceived failures behind. Our Lord's love is not contingent on your perfect performance; it is a limitless grace, freeing you to step back onto the field and rediscover the profound joy and purpose of your walk with the Lord.

Perhaps you don't identify as a believer at all, or maybe you carry a healthy dose of skepticism about organized religion. Do you sometimes find yourself disillusioned by the bitter political divisions, the empty pursuit of status on social media, or the overwhelming anxiety that modern life cultivates? Perhaps you've realized that the central promise of our age—that technology, affluence, and convenience would eventually bring lasting peace and genuine fulfillment—is, at its core, a falsehood. If you are weary of the noise and hungry for a foundation that resists the shifting cultural tides, this book offers a space for honest exploration. It is not here to preach, but to examine universal truths that lie beneath the surface of the chaos, offering a path toward a more meaningful reality, regardless of where your current convictions lie. If this describes where you are today, be assured that you are not alone in feeling lost.

We begin by acknowledging the common struggle: the exhausting pursuit of truth in a confusing world, the isolation fueled by a narcissistic digital culture, and the wounds left by our relentless political divisions. My aim is not to condemn these forces, but to thoughtfully dissect them to understand the deep longings they are attempting to satisfy within us. We will confront the resulting emptiness head-on, preparing the way to move beyond the void and toward authentic meaning. And then, we will pivot, as we share truth in Christ: Simply Christ.

This is where we stop chasing fleeting shadows and begin walking toward the light. We are going to examine the case for Jesus Christ with fresh eyes, demonstrating why His message is not an ancient relic, but the most radical, liberating, and relevant truth for your life *today*. He offers a redemption that cleanses, a joy that lasts, and a peace that makes sense of the chaos.

This is your invitation to an honest and urgent journey toward the narrow path that Jesus described, which leads to a lasting peace beyond what we can understand. We will dive deep into today's most pressing circumstances, presenting fresh, powerful insights into the breadth of God's love. This book is designed to challenge and galvanize believers into meaningful action, and to gently but firmly draw nonbelievers toward the hope of redemption.

If you are ready to trade anxiety for certainty and the noise of the world for the quiet assurance of God's truth, turn the page. The journey toward the narrow way begins now.

One:

THE NOISE AND THE NEED FOR PEACE

*I wrote **Beyond the Broad Path** because I believe that a reliable anchor exists and that truth is not dead; it is simply obscured.*

I was recently engaged in an intense discussion with an acquaintance regarding faith and the state of the world today. This person had broached the subject of religion, knowing I would not back away from the topic, and he was determined to discredit the Bible as nothing more than a collection of allegories and fables. My simple response was this: "The Bible, the collected Word of God, is truth." He immediately responded, almost shouting, "The Bible is **not** truth!" In fact, he repeated the statement twice for emphasis. What fascinated me wasn't the debate itself, but his powerful, almost visceral reaction to this single word: Truth.

Today, truth is regarded the same as beauty: It exists only in the eye of the beholder. What was once foundational and beyond reproach is measured on a sliding scale of subjective inference. We live in an era of unprecedented connectivity, yet we feel more disconnected than ever. This constant social and political friction leaves us exhausted because the ground beneath our feet feels unstable. Truth is the proverbial glue that holds nations together; without it, the concrete foundation of civil discourse is reduced to shifting sand. Consider this: If there is no truth, then there can be no lies.

Is Truth Dead?

This question poses a challenge to reality that is not new. In George Orwell's *1984*, he envisioned a dystopian nightmare experienced through his protagonist Winston Smith, a governmental everyman laboring away deep within the bowels of the Records Department at the Ministry of Truth. His work was both forthright and diabolical: to rewrite history or delete it altogether to eradicate any contradictions with the current statements of the elite. The result is a polished version of reality that corroborates the day's propaganda.

This scenario feels chillingly familiar. The truth in its purest form stands on its own merits—factual, indisputable, and verifiable. But the problem with indisputable truth is that it becomes terribly inconvenient when one side is determined to impose their will upon another. They justify their tools of subterfuge while utilizing a stratagem of deceit to achieve their goals, arguing that the outcome is of such vital importance that it justifies any violation of accuracy as being acceptable for the common good. This targeted cultural deception, this collective gaslighting, is designed to keep us perpetually anxious, fundamentally divided, and constantly chasing temporary certainties that never deliver lasting security. We are being trained to doubt our instincts and mistrust our neighbor.

We watch as foundations crumble, and we are left asking: Where is the reliable anchor in this storm? How can we discern objective reality when everyone claims a personal version of the truth, often weaponizing their claims?

I wrote *Beyond the Broad Path* because I believe that a reliable anchor exists and that truth is not dead; it is simply obscured. This book traces a journey to cut through the confusion, expose the fabricated narratives, and reconnect you with unshakable truths that have sustained humanity for millennia. We will not shy away from the hard realities of our world; instead, we will confront the global troubles we face—the crises of faith, purpose, and peace—and hold them up against the light of Scripture.

In the coming pages, I offer both critique and construction. This book declares that there are constants in a world of variables. We will shift from merely identifying the symptoms of our cultural sickness to presenting the antidote. We will provide biblical answers to life's most pressing questions, demonstrating with clarity and conviction that the hope you seek is not found in a fragile political ideology, a fleeting self-help trend, or the empty promises of a new digital doctrine. It's time to stop looking horizontally at the chaos and start looking vertically at the truth, which resides in the resurrected Savior, Jesus Christ.

To the Christian believer, this book is a challenge to stop retreating from the culture wars and boldly share the peace you have found. To the nonbeliever, this book is an invitation: a chance to examine the evidence, find the answers you've been looking for, and discover a new life that provides peace that surpasses all human understanding.

The Inconvenience of Truth

In Jesus's time on earth, his teachings of servant leadership and putting the needs of others above one's own self flew directly in the face of the establishment. Whenever someone stands up and dares to disrupt and dismantle the corrupt systems manipulated for self-pleasure, those systems will not idly stand by while their golden calf is slaughtered. The Pharisees schemed and plotted, behind closed doors, to kill the one who spoke truth.

When they arrested Jesus, their heinous plot was set in motion. The high priest questioned Jesus about his disciples and about his teaching:

> *"I have spoken openly to the world," Jesus answered him. "I have always taught in the synagogue and in the temple, where all the Jews gather, and I haven't spoken anything in secret. Why do you question me? Question those who heard what I told them. Look, they know what I said." When he had said these things, one of the officials standing by slapped Jesus, saying, "Is this the way you answer the high priest?" "If I have spoken wrongly," Jesus answered him, "give evidence about the wrong; but if rightly, why do you hit me?*
>
> —John 18:20–23 CSB

Later, they sent Jesus to be interrogated by the Roman prefect, Pontius Pilate. In reading these Scriptures, one thing is clear: Pilate was much like the politicians we elect and re-elect *ad nauseam.* He was ready to pontificate, convinced of his own grandiose abilities, yet when pressed to make the right and just decision, he chose the coward's way out. Pilate knew Jesus was an innocent man, having done nothing to merit arrest, let alone a punishment of death. But faced with a growing demand from the populace to crucify Jesus, he could not find it within himself to do what was right.

Pilate told them, "You take him and judge him according to your law." "It's not legal for us to put anyone to death," the Jews declared. . . . Then Pilate went back into the headquarters, summoned Jesus, and said to him, "Are you the king of the Jews?" . . . "My kingdom is not of this world," said Jesus. . . . You say that I'm a king," Jesus replied. "I was born for this, and I have come into the world for this: to testify to the truth. Everyone who is of the truth listens to my voice." "What is truth?" said Pilate.

—John 18:31–38 CSB

The Anchor of God's Perfect Will

As unexpected as this might seem, the ultimate failure of Pilate is exactly the reason all believers should be joyful and full of hope. These scriptures demonstrate how God's perfect plan of salvation was effectively administered according to His will: "*For God sent not his Son into the world to condemn the world; but that the world through him might be saved*" (John 3:17).

Consider this: What if the Governor of Judea had been a strong leader, full of courage and resolve, ready to rule with a swift hand of justice based in truth? Jesus would undoubtedly have been released to the Jewish leaders, who, under Roman law, were not allowed to carry out the death penalty. God's will is perfect, but here we have the benefit of hindsight. God had to allow Pontius Pilate to be in that position of authority at exactly that time for the perfect plan of salvation—Jesus's death on a cross—to be fulfilled, so that all mankind could be redeemed.

In understanding this method, through the study of Scripture, we can and should stand up with courage and face each day, filled with hope, knowing that God is in control. As I've heard it shared many times, "things are not falling apart, they are falling into place" according to God's plans. We are witnessing some of the greatest turmoil in recent history, but we need not look any further than the example of Pilate to see how God allows some officials to hold office to fulfill His will for mankind.

The Call to a Contrasting Life

Everyone who has accepted Jesus into their heart has no reason to shrink back and hide or sit in fear of some unknown danger lurking just around the corner. We have work to do; indeed, our best life is ahead of us. Get up, sing God's praises for another day, and go about your work with a happy countenance of peace.

The world is on a downward trajectory, with all forms of evil forces stepping out of the darkness into full public display. It is all too common to see violence in the streets, mass killings, anger, and a total loss of any semblance of self-control, all of which makes it perfectly clear that, because we are not of this world, our lives as Christians should stand in stark contrast, filled with peace and hope.

Be that light in this dark world so that others who might

be living in fear, not having the benefit of a personal relationship with God, will be drawn to that light that represents the love of Christ. This is your opportunity to be a living testimony to a life set apart from this fallen world. In closing, consider the context of Jesus's prayer in the Garden of Gethsemane on the very evening he would be betrayed:

> *Now I am coming to you, and I speak these things in the world so that they may have my joy completed in them. I have given them your word. The world hated them because they are not of the world, just as I am not of the world. I am not praying that you take them out of the world but that you protect them from the evil one. They are not of the world, just as I am not of the world. Sanctify them by the truth; your word is truth. As you sent me into the world, I also have sent them into the world. I sanctify myself for them, so that they also may be sanctified by the truth.*
>
> —John 17:13–19 CSB

We do not have to ask, "What is Truth?" The Word of God is Truth. John goes on to tell us that the Word became flesh and gave himself as a sacrifice for many. Jesus told us that he is "*the way, the truth and the life*" (John 14:16). Furthermore, Jesus said, "*He that is* ***not with me is against me, and he that gathereth not with me scattereth abroad***" (Matthew 12:30 emphasis added).

Study the words of Scripture and allow yourself to be

filled with joy and hope. Let the peace that surpasses all understanding guard your heart and mind. Do not let the evil in this world steal your joy—acknowledge God in all things and stand firm in truth.

Two:

AUTOCRATIC GASLIGHTING

This represents the shape-shifting, truth-bending dialogue the public has come to expect from our government entities, news media, public health officials. The verb *gaslighting* means:

> To psychologically manipulate (a person) usually over an extended period of time so that the victim questions the validity of their own thoughts, perception of reality, or memories and experiences confusion, loss of confidence and self-esteem, and doubts concerning their own emotional or mental stability: to subject (someone) to gaslighting.[1]

[1] *Merriam-Webster Dictionary*, "gaslight," accessed May 20, 2021, https://www.merriam-webster.com/dictionary/gaslight.

Gaslighting is certainly not a new concept. This form of misdirection has long been used to avoid the truth and create doubt by shifting the focus back on the one asking the questions, but it certainly has taken on wider application in recent years. A recent and striking example of this political theater occurred during public testimony regarding the origins of the COVID-19 global pandemic. When a high-ranking public health official was confronted with evidence of funding linked to controversial laboratory research, the dialogue mirrored the same shape-shifting tactics seen in decades past. Rather than providing a transparent accounting of the facts, the testimony dissolved into a calculated dispute over definitions.

Much like Bill Clinton's infamous "it depends on what the meaning of the word *is* is" from the 1990s, the COVID-19 defense relied on narrowing and re-defining technical terms to bypass the obvious truth. In both instances, the strategy was the same: When the facts are indefensible, change the meaning of the words used to describe them. This tactic is the essence of political gaslighting—an attempt to convince the public that what they see with their own eyes is merely a misunderstanding of vocabulary.

The Cost of Chaos: Living Unmoored

The deliberate twisting of facts, the constant shifting of narratives, and the relentless application of autocratic gaslighting achieves a terrifying objective: It robs the soul of certainty. When the foundations of civil discourse become shifting sand, human beings are left unmoored, adrift in a sea of anxiety and fear.

It is no coincidence that in this modern age of unprecedented material comfort and technological connection, anxiety and depression rates continue to skyrocket, especially among the young. If truth is simply subjective and if what was fact yesterday can be denied as entirely and completely incorrect today, how can anyone possibly build a stable life, a future, or even a secure identity?

We are inherently designed for truth. Our minds crave verifiable reality; our hearts yearn for constancy. When that fundamental need is continually frustrated by the very institutions meant to protect and inform us, the result is profound spiritual and emotional chaos. This chaos manifests not just in political polarization, but in personal exhaustion, fear of the future, and a deep, gnawing sense of instability.

The noise of the world is designed to overwhelm us, to prevent us from hearing the still, small voice of God. The objective of the **father of lies** (John 8:44) has always been to separate humanity from the Truth, because where Truth is absent, fear and bondage thrive.

The Global Agenda and Mass Confusion

The narrative has continued to shift in ways that appear to fit the political agenda of those seeking absolute control. The dialogue is not hidden. Simply search the internet for the term *World Economic Forum* (WEF) and the sweeping agenda known as "The Great Reset" is there for all to read. In fact, curiously but not surprisingly, you'll also find the term *Build Back Better* inserted in this narrative. Sound familiar? It should—that was the foundational pitch phrase used by the recent Biden administration during their run for office.

This global strategy or narrative is a well-funded and expertly organized movement that is being pushed by any means necessary. The ever-shifting narratives that surrounded the pandemic—false storylines, altered timelines, unending questions about masks, one COVID-19 shot or two shots or booster shots—were designed to cause doubt and mistrust. This mass confusion is a well-thought-out delivery meant to be autocratic gaslighting. It's a means to an end, and that end is worldwide control over every aspect of life as we know it. Achieving that outcome means that bending the rules, breaking the law, and outright lies are all tools to be used so long as they help drive the planned narrative in reaching the final objective.

The Blame Game and Weaponizing Fear

Gaslighting occurs when your emotions, words, and experiences are twisted and used against you, causing you to question reality. We saw this vividly regarding the question of vaccinations. Each person has the right to seek information and draw their own conclusions about what they allow into their body. Many were reluctant because this treatment used messenger ribonucleic acid, or mRNA for short, a technology never before deployed in mass vaccination efforts. Some were concerned because of the lack of data regarding possible long-term adverse effects; therefore it was reasonable for people to delay receiving the vaccine until more was known.

However, the right to make your own informed decision was deemed unacceptable. The media machine, in coordination and often under direction of potentially biased government authorities, set out to bombard the population with information that was often contradictory but pushed in such a way that resulted in sensory overload. Facts were twisted and the narrative was turned against the unvaccinated in ways intended to marginalize individuals with derogatory labels and other pressures that caused many to begin to question their own reality. Consider these examples:

- US Surgeon General says pandemic is spiraling out of control due to the unvaccinated.[2]
- Alabama Governor Ivey says, "Start blaming the unvaccinated folks"[3]

---

[2] Melissa Quinn, "Former Surgeon General Jerome Adams says, 'Pandemic Is Spiraling out of Control Again' Because of Unvaccinated Americans," CBS News, "Face the Nation," July 26, 2021, https://www.cbsnews.com/news/covid-pandemic-vaccines-jerome-adams/.

[3] CNN.com Wire Service, "Alabama Republican Gov. Ivey: "Start Blaming the Unvaccinated Folks," *The Mercury News*, July 23, 2021,

While the overall media narrative told us almost 100 percent of those hospitalized were unvaccinated, facts were harder to find. In early 2021, Reuters reported that almost half of all new COVID cases in Great Britain and 30 percent of COVID deaths were of fully vaccinated individuals. It just didn't add up; yet no one ever came forward to clarify. Then came the many variants, infecting both vaccinated and unvaccinated alike. Since it wasn't as simple as placing all blame on the unvaccinated, you must ask yourself: Why did they push that narrative? It became more about control and less about the virus. Was this a dry run of sorts, where those dark forces tested the narrative to see just how far this level of subservience from the masses could be achieved?

A very common tool of those who gaslight is the blame game. This frightening tactic is used worldwide to turn people against each other. Labeling and name-calling ramp up the pressure, and many eventually give up and go along rather than face the onslaught of accusations or consequences that result from their resistance.

Weaponizing Faith: A Tactic of the Enemy

Another tool used is to speak in terms that are endeared by those they wish to influence or change. We saw this tactic

---

https://www.mercurynews.com/2021/07/23/alabama-gov-ivey-start-blaming-the-unvaccinated-folks/.

when, after singling out "evangelicals" and "patriots," then Vice-President Kamala Harris quoted Scripture to marginalize the "deplorables" while solidifying her base of supporters: "I do believe that the act of getting vaccinated is the very essence—the very essence—of what the Bible tells us when it says, 'love thy neighbor.'"[4]

It is often wise to exercise caution when politicians across the political spectrum integrate Bible verses into policy arguments. This politically motivated use of theology can become a troubling trend, often viewed as misleading or self-serving when leveraged to justify a specific political agenda. An example from 2021 involved the vice-president citing Scripture in a public health appeal, which some interpreted as an attempt to shame citizens into vaccination. This raised questions among critics about the selective application of religious teachings in the political arena, particularly given the administration's stances on other issues often addressed by those same texts.

The perceived inconsistency between a politician's personal or policy stances and their public use of biblical references can be interpreted by critics as a significant breach of rhetorical integrity. This blending of moralistic appeals with seemingly self-serving political goals often suggests a

[4] "Kamala Harris Delivers Remarks at Vaccine Center," PBS News video, Detroit, Michigan, July 11, 2021, https://www.pbs.org/newshour/politics/watch-live-harris-delivers-remarks-at-vaccine-center-in-detroit-michigan.

high degree of confidence in the speaker's own position. For many religious observers, this behavior echoes a significant theological lesson found in Scripture regarding the misapplication of sacred text. The account is found in Matthew 4:1–11, where Satan attempts to misuse Scripture to tempt Jesus; this is a powerful reminder of how even familiar verses can be extracted from their proper context and deployed to justify actions that are contrary to their intended meaning. This raises serious questions about the ethical deployment of faith in the political sphere.

Crippling Costs: Discontent and Division

The result of this psychological and political warfare is not just personal anxiety, but a breakdown of communal life. Without a foundation in absolute Truth, all arguments become matters of personal will and power, not of reason or reconciliation. This is the seed of discontent and division that is now crippling our world.

Discontent is fostered by the constant shifting of goals and the promise of endless, unfulfilling material or political liberation. When the definitions of success, justice, and even gender are fluid and dictated by an elite authority, the average person is left scrambling, feeling inadequate or "on the wrong side" of history. The gnawing feeling that "something is wrong," but you can't quite name it is the intended outcome of gaslighting.

This deep dissatisfaction fuels division. The forces

seeking autocratic control know that a house divided cannot stand. By magnifying differences—whether political, racial, or medical—and encouraging the blame game, they ensure that the masses are too busy fighting each other to ever look up and challenge the real source of the oppression. We are told to hate our neighbors because they voted differently, to distrust the person in the next pew because they made a different health choice, or to view history as a weapon to destroy our shared heritage.

But the spiritual battle being fought for this division is not new. The world will always try to force us into opposing camps, but Christ commands unity, love, and service. This manufactured strife is simply the latest manifestation of the enemy's ancient strategy: to scatter abroad. The only enduring antidote to this widespread discontent and crippling division is a commitment to the unwavering, unifying truth found only in the gospel.

The Call to Hope and Urgent Action

> *And because iniquity shall abound, the love of many shall wax cold. But he that shall endure unto the end shall be saved. And this gospel of the kingdom shall be preached in all the world for a witness unto all nations; and then shall the end come.*
>
> —Matthew 24:12–14

We see it all around us: Lawlessness abounds. So, how do we guard our hearts and minds? Through our faith in Jesus Christ, the one without sin, God in the flesh, who came to this earth not to condemn the world, but to save it. He gave his life as a ransom for many.

But know this and heed the warning: Jesus will return as promised. That return will bring with it the full judgment and consequences that will go to those who denied God and refused His gift of salvation. This age of subterfuge perpetrated by those seeking to gain worldwide control is just the beginning of what is to come. Recently, it was the opportunistic use of the pandemic to remove individual rights; tomorrow it may well be the call to bow to one leader, to take his mark; otherwise, you will not be able to buy or sell, and your very life will be required of you if you resist. The church will be gone, but for those left behind, Daniel's prophesied "Time of Jacob's trouble" will go from bad to worse.

That is why our message is urgent; we do not want anyone to miss the opportunity to come to know Jesus before it is too late.

> *If you declare with your mouth, "Jesus is Lord," and believe in your heart that God raised him from the dead, you will be saved. For it is with your heart that you believe and are justified, and it is with your mouth that you profess your faith and are saved.*
>
> —Romans 10:9–10 NIV

To the faithful: Are you evangelizing according to our shared calling from Jesus? If you truly believe that you have been saved through grace and that Jesus Christ died for all sinners, then step up and share that message! The world is lost, and we are the light, but if we hide that light under a bushel then what good are we? Share the gospel, as Charles Spurgeon exhorted, "anywhere and everywhere!" We should feel anguish in our hearts to know that "*narrow is the gate and few will find it.*" Get involved, don't wait for someone else to take up the charge, follow our Lord's instructions and lead the way.

I conclude with the reminder, we do not have to ask, "What is truth?" The Word of God is truth. Let that peace that surpasses all understanding guard your heart and mind. Do not let the evil within this world steal your joy; acknowledge God in all things and stand firm in truth.

Three:

THE PEACE THAT GUARDS THE HEART AND MIND

God's peace is freely offered, but it comes with a commitment that runs directly counter to the world's agenda of self-gratification.

We began this journey by asking: Is truth dead? And through examining the systemic chaos of autocratic gaslighting, we found that the answer for the world is a resounding yes. The result is a population adrift, crippled by anxiety and division, desperately searching for an anchor that the world simply cannot provide.

The good news—the gospel—is that we are not meant

to live in that confusion. We have been granted an internal defense system against external storms. This defense is the promise of Christ, beautifully captured in a single, powerful passage of Scripture that addresses the very anxiety plaguing our modern age:

> *Do not be anxious about anything, but in every situation, by prayer and petition, with thanksgiving, present your requests to God. And the peace of God, which transcends all understanding, will guard your hearts and your minds in Christ Jesus.*
>
> —Philippians 4:6–7 NIV

A Peace That Surpasses

This promise is more than just a tranquil feeling or a pleasant emotion; it is a profound act of spiritual protection. The Greek word Paul uses for guard (*phrourēsō*) is a military term. It means to garrison or station soldiers around a city or fortress to repel attacks.

Think of your heart and mind as a fortress under constant siege. The attacks come not only from the lies and noise of the world, but from the spiritual forces that feed the anxiety, doubt, and fear we detailed in the last chapter. This world is actively trying to infiltrate your thoughts and steal your joy.

When you heed Paul's instruction to trade anxiety for prayer and petition with thanksgiving, God promises to station His divine peace around your innermost being. This peace acts as a celestial sentry, standing watch against the barrage of shifting narratives and fear-based headlines. It is a peace that surpasses understanding because it is completely illogical. It allows a believer to stand calm and certain in the middle of worldwide turmoil, a phenomenon no philosophy or political ideology can ever replicate.

Jesus Calms the Storm: Peace in the Crisis

"*Thy word is a lamp unto my feet, and a light unto my path*" (Psalms 119:105).

We often find ourselves yearning for a sense of equilibrium in a world defined by constant turmoil. The persistent clamor of competing narratives, the currents of anger and animosity, and the relentless pressure of personal and collective crises can make life feel like a storm without a harbor. When you are overwhelmed, the search for a true refuge and lasting sense of peace becomes paramount.

The Gospel of Mark offers a profound illustration of transcendent calm and ultimate authority in the account of Jesus calming the storm:

And there arose a great storm of wind, and the waves beat into the ship, so that it was now full. And he was in the hinder part of the ship, asleep on a pillow: and they awake him, and say unto him, Master, carest thou not that we perish? And he arose, and rebuked the wind, and

> *said unto the sea, Peace, be still. And the wind ceased, and there was a great calm. And he said unto them, Why are ye so fearful? how is it that ye have no faith? And they feared exceedingly, and said one to another, What manner of man is this, that even the wind and the sea obey him?*
>
> —Mark 4:37–41

This narrative is not merely a historical event, but a powerful spiritual analogy. The vessel represents the human experience, tossed by the external and internal anxieties that threaten to capsize us. Jesus's ability to command the elements with three simple words, "Peace, be still," demonstrates a sovereignty that extends beyond physical forces to the very core of our fears. For believers, this passage underscores the conviction that a source of unshakable stability exists, even when life's crises seem inescapable. It challenges the reader to consider the object of their trust when the storms of life begin to rage, suggesting that true inner peace is found not in the absence of turmoil, but in the presence of an authority that transcends it.

Finding Peace and Facing Commitment

The preceding illustration of Christ commanding the storm serves as a powerful reminder of divine sovereignty—a theological assurance that even amid life's most turbulent periods, a transcendent power maintains control. For the believer, this narrative instills the conviction that fear is unnecessary, as Jesus remains present and ready to intervene, always acting within the loving will of the heavenly Father. It also offers a realistic perspective: Storms are inevitable, regardless of one's spiritual proximity to God. Yet, the peace promised is not the absence of trouble, but rather a profound inner tranquility that can be accessed amid the trial, rooted in the certainty that God is attentive to our challenges and guiding our lives according to His purpose.

The Cost of Peace: Denying the Self

While divine peace is freely offered, the commitment required to fully embrace it often runs counter to the world's prevailing values of autonomy and self-gratification. This commitment is the true cost of discipleship.

This tension between worldly desire and spiritual dedication is a common theme in the journey of faith. Recently, someone shared with me the experience of witnessing to a friend who expressed belief in Jesus but felt unable to commit to salvation. The hesitation stemmed from a recognition that accepting Christ would necessitate a fundamental change in lifestyle—a yielding of worldly attachments or habits. This individual understood that faith demanded a profound shift in priority, and they were not yet prepared to make that commitment.

This scenario highlights a common reluctance many individuals face: the apprehension of surrendering the familiar comforts and self-determined trajectory of life. Jesus addresses this requirement for commitment with perfect clarity, defining the very nature of following Him:

> *Then said Jesus unto his disciples, If any man will come after me, let him deny himself, and take up his cross, and follow me. For whosoever will save his life shall lose it: and whosoever will lose his life for my sake shall find it. For what is a man profited, if he shall gain the whole world, and lose his own soul? or what shall a man give in exchange for his soul?*
>
> —Matthew 16:24–26

This passage presents a stark dichotomy between the temporal and the eternal. Jesus does not obscure the difficulty of the path; rather, He defines Christian following as an act of self-renunciation (denying the self) and a courageous acceptance of one's designated burdens (taking up the cross). The central challenge is the willingness to exchange the pursuit of a temporary, self-directed life for a life of purpose found in obedience to God. The rhetorical question ("*For what is a man profited, if he shall gain the whole world, and lose his own soul?*") forces every potential disciple to weigh the ultimate value of their choices, underscoring that the pursuit of spiritual peace requires a conscious surrender of ego and worldly ambition.

The Necessity of Commitment and the Path of the Cross

It is crucial to acknowledge the concept of singularity within the Christian call to discipleship: There is a necessary clarity of allegiance. The scriptural teaching suggests that a life cannot be equally devoted to worldly pursuits and to the divine kingdom; a clear choice between the two is required. Jesus issues a solemn warning regarding this decision, indicating that failing to acknowledge and live by His identity in this earthly life has eternal consequences in one's standing before God the Father.

The path of the cross is explicitly defined as challenging—a rugged journey that demands self-denial. This requirement necessitates a continuous commitment to relinquish the desires, comforts, and ambitions of the world that compete with the priority of following Christ.

Following the Via Dolorosa

This commitment is powerfully symbolized by Christ's own journey of suffering. We remember Jesus, scourged and wounded, carrying the rough, splintered wood of His cross along the *Via Dolorosa* (the Way of Suffering), leading ultimately to His crucifixion on Calvary.

The command to "*take up our cross daily and follow me*" is therefore an invitation to participate in that same spirit of sacrifice and surrendered will. It is a continuous act of placing our complete faith and trust in God, sealed by the central conviction of the Christian faith, acknowledging that Jesus was raised from the dead thereby offering salvation and eternal reconciliation.

The road of discipleship is undeniably difficult; it often demands opposition to cultural norms and the subjugation of personal will. However, the spiritual reward—the gift of eternity promised through this difficult path—is presented as infinitely outweighing the cost. The sacrifice demanded is steep, but the ultimate prize is defined as priceless.

The Final Call: Choosing Peace Over the Storm

Considering the magnitude of life's turbulence, Christ's offering of lasting peace, underscored by His ultimate act of self-giving, is the most significant act in the history of mankind. This peace is not dependent on worldly circumstances but is rooted in the depth of His sacrifice for humanity.

We are called to a moment of honest self-reflection. A candid assessment often reveals that despite all efforts to fill the emptiness with temporary gratifications—whether through success, comfort, or material gain—a persistent void remains in the human spirit. The relentless search for fulfillment apart from a spiritual center can be exhausting.

Addressing the Barriers to Faith

For those who hesitate, the resistance is often multi-faceted. Perhaps the current landscape of the institutional church, with its perceived flaws and inconsistencies (which we previously analyzed in the political sphere), acts as a deterrent. Or perhaps there is a sense of social apprehension— a feeling of not "fitting in" with the traditional church community. I encourage you to temporarily set these external barriers aside. The core reward of accepting Jesus as Savior is not immediate social integration, but the initiation of a daily, personal walk with Him. This relationship is the primary focus, and as this commitment deepens, the ancillary concerns and external anxieties begin to diminish, leading to full and unconditional acceptance within the family of God.

The Urgency of the Eternal

Do not continue to be held captive by the deception that the temporary pursuits of this world offer lasting satisfaction. Your soul possesses intrinsic and eternal importance too significant to risk trading for fleeting worldly gains, which lead to an eternal separation from the divine source of life.

The world is marked by strife, political contention, and moral ambiguity, which clearly reflect the instability we first described as a raging storm. This visible turmoil serves as a sobering reminder of the impending urgency for spiritual clarity. The Scriptures suggest that the day will come when

God gathers those who have placed their faith in Jesus, leaving the world in a vacuum of spiritual darkness.

The storm is indeed raging, visibly evident in the anxieties and conflicts of our age. There is no time left for procrastination. The moment to choose stability, refuge, and peace is now. As we continue through the remaining chapters, for those who have not yet made a profession of faith in Christ, I offer many opportunities to face this most important decision, and I implore you to call out to Jesus and allow His authority to settle the chaos in your heart, echoing His powerful command over the sea: "*Peace, be still.*"

Four:

THE GREAT DIVIDE: THE WAR FOR ALLEGIANCE

How does the feel-good verbosity of the prosperity message and the "Be your best self" grandiloquence find any commonality with a faith that requires you to deny self and take up a cross to follow our Lord Jesus?

If you have answered the call to follow Christ, denying yourself and accepting the peace that surpasses all understanding, you have secured your fortress. However, stepping outside that fortress requires confronting a stark reality: The world is not merely anxious; it is engaged in a profound and escalating civil war. The spiritual battle we have alluded to manifests daily as a growing, bitter ideological divide—a fundamental fracture—that cripples communities, families, and nations.

This is not simply a squabble between political parties or cultural preferences. It is a war for allegiance, a battle of worldviews between the shifting sand of relativistic humanism and the bedrock of divine truth.

More Than Politics: Two Spiritual Kingdoms

The division we witness today feels uniquely destructive because it is fueled by a spiritual darkness that demands total conformity and brooks no disagreement. When truth is subjective, as we explored earlier, everything becomes a tool for power. People are no longer seen as individuals made in God's image, but as members of constantly warring identity groups. Dialogue is replaced by accusation, and empathy is shattered by antagonism.

This current reality should surprise no believer, for Christ himself declared the necessary consequence of choosing truth:

> *Do not suppose that I have come to bring peace to the earth. I did not come to bring peace, but a sword. For I have come to turn a man against his father, a daughter against her mother, a daughter-in-law against her mother-in-law—a man's enemies will be the members of his own household.*
>
> —Matthew 10:34–36 NIV

This sword is not one of violence, but one of separation. When Christ enters a life, He establishes an absolute standard of righteousness that immediately conflicts with the relative standards of a fallen world. The natural man lives by the world's truth, and the spiritual man lives by God's truth. When those two worldviews exist in the same home, community, or culture, friction is inevitable.

This chapter will unmask the modern forms this ideological war takes and provide the biblical perspective necessary to navigate them without losing your peace or compromising your faith.

The Prophetic Divide: A Spiritual Watershed

The Continental Divide, also known as The Great Divide, extends from northern Alaska southward across North America, then continues through Central and finally South America where it ends. This prominent divide of the continent, in very basic terms, separates the hydrological features and watersheds, thus forming the pattern of the rivers while influencing the runoff toward the Pacific and Atlantic oceans. While there are several lesser divides in North America, this Great Divide, as it is known, represents the primary divide across the entire continent.

In today's world a prophetic divide is growing, separating the spiritual realms, a tug-of-war between good and evil that will determine the flow of humanity toward its final destination for all eternity. This reality should be of little surprise to anyone, whether a believer or not, as interest in end times prophecy has grown in earnest over recent decades pointing toward the rapture of the church and the coming tribulation. Ironically, as signs are revealed at an unprecedented rate, many a pulpit has chosen to look the other way as opposed to preaching this most important message in these perilous times. Whether that message is accepted or not is up to the listener, but keep in mind that God has always demonstrated great patience and gives warnings so that all creation might be saved. But that patience will run out, and consequences will follow: "*The Lord does not delay his promise, as some understand delay, but is patient with you, not wanting any to perish but all to come to repentance*" (2 Peter 3:9 CSB).

Before the great flood, there were warnings for many decades, but humanity in general ignored the call to righteousness; the consequences were devastating. Likewise with Sodom and Gomorrah, warnings went unheeded, indulgence in all forms of depravity became the norm, and the consequences soon followed. Now today, the warnings are prevalent; God has gone to great lengths through the many prophecies given in His Word to alert the world to turn back from evil as the end is drawing near, but the great majority do not want to hear it.

Compromise and the True Cost of Discipleship

The spiritual divide is growing, both within the church and in the wider world, leading to eternal decisions that are irreversible once the door to redemption closes. Globally, many denominations are compromising the Word of God to appease an increasingly intolerant mindset among the masses—either to avoid persecution or simply to align with contemporary trends. They celebrate their own version of tolerance while sharing a message of lies through omission by failing to teach the entire gospel. This raises a critical question: If the core message of the church is compromised, what is its purpose? If we cannot address the reality of sin, there is no need for a Savior and, therefore, no point to the church's existence.

Persecution of those who stand firmly in the truth of Scripture is coming; Jesus made that very clear, and He also defined the expectations of a true follower. I challenge all believers to compare His words with what you see and hear in your church. If the two don't align, you have to speak up and question the message and find the truth.

> *Blessed are they which are persecuted for righteousness' sake: for theirs is the kingdom of heaven. Blessed are ye, when men shall revile you, and persecute you, and shall say all manner of evil against you falsely, for my sake. Rejoice, and be exceeding glad: for great is your reward*

in heaven: for so persecuted they the prophets which were before you. Ye are the salt of the earth: but if the salt have lost his savour, wherewith shall it be salted? it is thenceforth good for nothing, but to be cast out, and to be trodden under foot of men. Ye are the light of the world. A city that is set on an hill cannot be hid. Neither do men light a candle, and put it under a bushel, but on a candlestick; and it giveth light unto all that are in the house. Let your light so shine before men, that they may see your good works, and glorify your Father which is in heaven.

—Matthew 5:10–16

How does the feel-good verbosity of the prosperity message and the "Be your best self" grandiloquence find any commonality with a faith that requires you to deny self and take up a cross to follow our Lord Jesus? The answer: It doesn't—period.

Reframing Global Turmoil: The Analogy of Birth Pains

The global community is currently experiencing a period characterized by heightened instability, conflict, and widespread societal distress. For many faith-based observers, these accumulating crises resonate strongly with the biblical concept of birth pains and prophetic signs described in the New Testament to signal the imminent culmination of the age and the inevitable return of Christ.

A Call to Critical Analysis

In light of this theological context, it is prudent to dedicate time here to a measured consideration of the modern political landscape. By closely examining the major developments unfolding around us such as shifts in international power dynamics, pervasive geopolitical instability, and the rise of unique ideological challenges, we can better gauge the potential biblical implications of these events. This analytical approach seeks to move beyond mere sensationalism, instead using Scripture as a sovereign framework to understand the trajectory and ultimate significance of current events, preparing observers not for fear, but for spiritual readiness.

The Shifting Sands of Afghanistan

The tumultuous withdrawal of the United States from Afghanistan created a vacuum that led to a swift and dramatic geopolitical realignment. While many Western nations, including France, Poland, and Germany, prioritized the immediate evacuation of embassy personnel and allied Afghan support workers, a notable counter-response emerged from other world powers.

China, Russia, and Turkey elected to maintain a presence, signaling a distinct posture toward the emerging political environment. China, for instance, announced its readiness to cooperate with Afghanistan's new governing entity, framing the shift as an internal matter for the Afghan people to determine. Simultaneously, reports indicated Russian diplomatic facilities were being secured by the advancing forces, and Turkey reiterated its commitment to sustained involvement within the country. This coordinated decision by these three nations not only to remain in-country, but to publicly express their intentions to engage with the new leadership, which is designated by the United Nations as a terror organization, stands as a compelling geopolitical indicator. It suggests a strategic and perhaps eager embrace of the shifting power structure in the region.

Analyzing the Alliance in Light of Ezekiel 38

This convergence of interests takes on profound significance for those who analyze current events through the lens of biblical prophecy. It invites a compelling comparison with the alliance described in Ezekiel chapter 38, which details the armies and lands destined to gather against Israel in the last days.

A careful examination of the geographical names referenced in the prophecy reveals striking correlations to the nations recently active in the Afghan sphere:

- **Rosh and Magog:** These terms have been extensively researched and are often associated with the territories of the former Soviet Union, encompassing modern-day Russia, and potentially regions including Afghanistan and territories north of the Black Sea.

- **Meshech and Tubal:** These lands are frequently linked by scholars to portions of modern-day Turkey, southern Russia, and the broader Anatolian region.
- **Persia:** Explicitly named, this territory historically encompassed Iran and extended into areas that include parts of Afghanistan and Pakistan.

The recent, almost simultaneous alignment of Russia, Turkey, and China (China is often associated with the "kings of the East" theme found in Revelation) in a region bordering these historical prophetic lands suggests that the conditions necessary for the formation of the Ezekiel-38-alliance may be rapidly taking shape. These geopolitical movements serve as an urgent reminder that, according to biblical eschatology, the final conflict may be drawing near.

The Failure of Leadership and the Rise of Rhetoric

In contemporary politics, the pursuit of accountability has often been replaced by a cycle of finger-pointing and blame-shifting. This dynamic has allowed a surge of partisan rhetoric to dominate the public sphere. Instead of offering substantive solutions, many elected officials prioritize deflecting responsibility, creating a political environment where quick soundbites overshadow genuine leadership.

The Problem of Partisan Maneuvering

Politics has devolved into a theater of masks, where survival of the power structure is the only true conviction. When a legacy figure defects to a rival camp, it is rarely an act of conscience; more often, it is a desperate bid for relevance. These spectacles inevitably spawn investigative panels that masquerade as justice but operate as engines of revenge—one side merely avenging a loss against the other. This cycle of retribution stands in stark contrast to the ministry of Jesus, which offered no such performance. Where politics builds on the shifting sands of public image and personal vendetta, His ministry established a bedrock of moral guidance and foundational truth intended for every soul, not just a favored party.

Deflecting Responsibility for Policy Failure

This theater of deflection reaches its height during moments of institutional failure. When long-standing policies collapse, those in power instinctively pivot, casting all blame onto their immediate predecessors. This strategy relies on a convenient collective amnesia—ignoring the fact that during previous eras of influence, these same leaders often presided over the very systems they now condemn. This selective memory reveals a deep lack of political integrity; it is a performance designed to preserve the self rather than solve the crisis. While political systems thrive on shifting blame, the path of Christ invites us to an honest reckoning with our own failures, meeting our transgressions not with condemnation, but with an atoning grace rooted in the eternal consistency of our heavenly Father.

The Spiritual Battle and the Specter of Globalism

The political and social turmoil detailed in this chapter—from the misuse of Scripture by leaders to the strategic realignments of global powers—must be understood within the context of an ongoing, transcendent struggle. The Apostle Paul articulated this battle with profound clarity, warning believers against focusing solely on human conflict: "*For we wrestle not against flesh and blood, but against principalities, against powers, against the rulers of the darkness of this world, against spiritual wickedness in high places* (Ephesians 6:12).

This passage compels us to recognize that the discord and deception we observe are rooted not merely in human failure, but in dark spiritual forces operating behind the visible machinations of the world. This is the spiritual battle, a conflict waged for the soul of humanity, utilizing the tools of political rhetoric, selective morality, and global instability.

The Rhetoric of a Unified World

In recent years, the language emerging from highly influential entities, such as the World Economic Forum (WEF), has lent a compelling contemporary urgency to this spiritual warning. Prominent discussions frequently advocate for principles of "Global Governance," a "Great Reset," and a deeply intertwined one-world alliance portrayed as essential to solving global crises such as climate change and pandemics.

While framed as solutions for stability and collective prosperity, this persistent push for unprecedented international consolidation and control points toward a scenario that is logically consistent with biblical eschatology. The desire for a centralized, unified global system—one that seeks to harmonize all political, economic, and social structures—could, by its very nature, set the definitive stage for a single, charismatic, and powerful human leader to emerge.

The Final Warning

This is the ultimate warning embedded within the Scriptures: The establishment of a one-world system capable of exercising total control over global commerce and culture is explicitly predicted to usher in the reign of the antichrist. The current geopolitical "birth pains," combined with the increasing momentum toward global unification, serve as a wake-up call for spiritual discernment.

We must remain vigilant, analyzing the world's rhetoric and crises not as random events, but as markers in the ongoing spiritual war. The choice remains simple, but the consequences are eternal: Place one's faith in the fleeting promises of a unified world system or hold fast to the unshakable sovereignty and offered peace of Jesus Christ.

Five:

THE UNMASKING OF INIQUITY: LAWLESSNESS AND THE DEEPENING DARKNESS

Today, truth is treated like beauty: It exists in the eye of the beholder. What once was foundational and beyond reproach is measured on a sliding scale of subjective inference.

In chapter 4, we examined the prophetic Great Divide, where ideological conflict and geopolitical alignments reveal a growing spiritual war for allegiance. But what is the immediate, palpable cost of this widening rift between the kingdom of God and the kingdoms of this world? It is the visible, daily, and terrifying increase in raw iniquity—a term encompassing lawlessness, malice, and cruelty.

The chaos of autocratic gaslighting gives way to social savagery. When objective truth is abandoned, the moral guardrails of civilization are removed, and the natural consequence is an explosion of evil. This reality was foretold by our Lord, giving us a clear metric for the approach of the end times: "*And because iniquity shall abound, the love of many shall wax cold* (Matthew 24:12).

The "*love of many shall wax cold*" is not a metaphor; it is the observable breakdown of community, empathy, and respect for human life that we see accelerate globally. It manifests not just in political disagreements but in cold, calculated, and often random acts of malice.

The Surge of Violence and the Spirit of the Age

We see this chilling effect in the normalization of violence. Whether it is mass shootings, the casual brutality on our streets, the rise of human trafficking, or the complete devaluation of life in the womb, society is shedding the moral constraints rooted in the Judeo-Christian ethic. What was once universally deemed horrific is now debated, tolerated, or even celebrated. The human heart, having rejected the light of Christ, naturally becomes a vessel for the deepening darkness.

However, among the many forms of evil rising today, one stands apart in its persistence, intensity, and sheer prophetic significance: antisemitism.

Antisemitism: The Eternal War Against God's People

The hatred directed at the Jewish people is not a sociological phenomenon; it is a spiritual mandate of the enemy. It is the most consistent and demonic form of hatred in human history, specifically because it targets the very people through whom God brought the Savior, Jesus Christ, into the world.

If Satan can successfully erase or annihilate Israel, he attacks the very root of God's plan of redemption. It is the eternal plot to frustrate the promises of the Old Testament and undermine the lineage of the Messiah. The current, alarming resurgence of antisemitism, masked in political rhetoric but fueled by the spirit of the antichrist, serves as one of the clearest markers that the final chapters of human history are being written. It is an unmasking of pure, raw evil, confirming the profound prophetic warnings we discussed in the preceding sections. The English poet A. E. Housman's word picture is *apropos*:[5]

> The signal-fires of warning
> They blaze, but none regard;
> And on through night to morning
> The world runs ruinward.

---

[5] A. E. Housman,

Why do evil, immorality, despair, and hopelessness seem so prevalent today? The overt hatred of the Jewish people and the nation of Israel is at or beyond the levels seen during Hitler's evil reign throughout World War II. Many are attempting to hide their raging antisemitism behind a thinly veiled facade of some newfound support for Palestine, but make no mistake, this is hatred of a people based solely upon their identity.

The Bible foretells of the days in which we live; Jesus Himself told of these things in Matthew 24:3–14 where He explained that "*these things must take place*" as they are part of the end of times. To say the world is out of control is not correct in this context because the Bible teaches that our current plight is part of God's eternal plans. The world has been building toward this time for centuries as many have turned away from God—even scoffed at His very existence, and God has given them over to their own evil desires. I'm not talking about political or corporate worldviews; I'm talking about the human condition at its very core. Unlike any time in the last several centuries, truth itself has been removed; we have no foundation upon which to stand in the public discourse. I once wrote, "without truth, there can be no lies," but given the fast pace of biblical prophecies fulfilled, one day soon, very soon, truth will be removed from this world, and woe to those left behind. A world without truth will be a world of lies governed by the father of lies.

October 7, 2023: The Unveiling of Raw Evil

That day, the world's moral equilibrium was shattered, as the scale of unprecedented atrocities revealed a disturbing shift in the tolerance for violence. Carried out by Hamas, a proxy terrorist organization, the attack saw the calculated brutality of evil step horrifyingly into the light. The methodical crimes against humanity—including the rape, beheading, and burning alive of elderly, infants, and women—defy adequate description, etching indelible trauma onto the collective memory. Amid the initial shock, the response was one of profound, universal sorrow and solidarity with the victims. Yet, the tragedy quickly gave way to a staggering moral paradox. As the affected community began the impossible task of mourning and resilience, a portion of the global public—even within Western democracies—chose to ignore the documented facts. Instead of denunciation, there has been a swift and disturbing re-emergence of global antisemitism, manifested by those who, with a troubling lack of contextual understanding, rush to blame the victims for the terror inflicted upon them.

The Erosion of Factual Reporting

The traditional ideal of objective journalism—the detached presentation of verifiable facts—has, for many observers, been superseded by agenda-driven narratives. Today, opinion and advocacy frequently masquerade as impartial, fact-based reporting. This shift often contributes to a widespread sense that the mainstream media narrative is being shaped by forces promoting a specific worldview, leading to a critical breakdown in trust between the public and media institutions.

The Climate of Intolerance

This atmosphere is further intensified by an intolerant spirit of intellectual vengeance, which often stifles genuine debate. Public conversation often presents a stark dichotomy: one must either align with the prevailing narrative, the "mainstream consensus," or risk becoming the target of an oppressive voice that seems to control substantial segments of media, entertainment, and news platforms. This dynamic creates a climate in which the pursuit of genuine justice and objective truth is compromised. Observers frequently note a reversal of moral and logical standards, where established concepts of right and wrong are blurred or inverted.

However, questioning the prevailing cultural and political agenda carries significant risk. Individuals who dare to challenge the consensus or the established narrative often face intense pressure, ostracization, or professional consequences. This situation underscores the challenge of maintaining both intellectual freedom and moral integrity in a world that increasingly demands conformity to a rapidly shifting ideological standard. "*Woe unto them that call evil good, and good evil, who put darkness for light and light for darkness, that put bitter for sweet, and sweet for bitter*" (Isaiah 5:20)!

Dr. Martin Luther King Jr. said:

> Darkness cannot drive out darkness; only light can do that. Hate cannot drive out hate; only love can do that. Hate multiplies hate, violence multiplies violence . . . in a descending spiral of destruction. . . . The chain reaction of evil–hate begetting hate, wars producing more wars must be broken, or we shall be plunged into the dark abyss of annihilation.[6]

God is love, and as our heavenly Father, it is very important to understand why we are given this paternal reference in our spiritual relationship to the Creator. Being the perfect Father to mankind, God does not lay out boundaries, laws, and guidelines to punish us; on the contrary, He sets boundaries as any good parent would. He knows the traps that await us, and He directs us away from those things that will ultimately destroy our souls should we choose certain paths in life. His is an all-encompassing love, a sacrificial selfless love; knowing we are born into a sinful and fallen world, this love provides redemption through Christ's ultimate sacrifice that is accompanied by God's written Word, which guides us through life with protections built in so that we may avoid

---

[6] Martin Luther King Jr, *Strength to Love* (Harper and Row, 1963), 141.

the destructive and damaging consequences of our own sinful nature.

Society continues to introduce changes that redefine the structure, concept, beliefs, and commonly held practices without performing unbiased evaluations of those changes. Furthermore, we remove God from the public spaces, yet we neglect to go back and validate the outcomes across the society. Then we are left to wonder what has gone so wrong in our world.

Today, truth is treated like beauty; that is, it exists in the eye of the beholder. What once was foundational, beyond question, is measured on a sliding scale of subjective inference. Truth is the proverbial glue that holds nations together; without truth, the concrete foundation of civil discourse is reduced to shifting sand.

Six:

THE CORRUPT CALCULUS OF POWER: WHEN LEADERS JUSTIFY THE MEANS

We must understand that so many around us do not know the truth of the gospel and, if we don't share the good news of salvation, who will?

We have established the prophetic reality: The world is divided into two spiritual kingdoms. In chapter 5, we examined the terrifying symptoms of this division—lawlessness, the decline of truth, and the surge of antisemitism. Now, we must turn our attention to the agents of that division, the leaders who actively manufacture discontent and employ any tactic necessary to maintain their control.

The average person feels a deep, corrosive sense of betrayal. The anxiety and chaos that cripple our world are not accidental; they are the intentional outcome of a leadership philosophy that has utterly abandoned moral constraints. We are not just divided by fate; we are being divided by design.

The New Machiavellianism: The End Justifies the Means

The guiding philosophy of this contemporary leadership crisis is nothing new. It is the core tenet of Niccolò Machiavelli's sixteenth-century work, *The Prince*, which argues that in politics, the morality of an action is judged only by its outcome. In other words, the ends justify the means.

For modern leaders—whether in government, media, corporate boardrooms, or even compromised religious structures—power and control are the only true moral objectives. In their quest to achieve their utopian or globalist agenda, they are willing to:

- **Manufacture division** (pitting race against race, rich against poor, one ideology against another).
- **Destroy objective truth** (gaslighting, fake news, information control).

- **Engage in hypocrisy and deceit** (publicly advocating virtue while privately practicing vice).

Not only are they willing to use these means, but they view them as politically necessary and even virtuous in service of their "greater good." This philosophy stands in absolute opposition to the standards set by Christ, where the means are as vital as the ends. God demands that we walk in integrity, righteousness, and truth, regardless of the cost. The world's leaders demand that you sacrifice integrity for the sake of power.

The Source of Discontent: Self-Serving Shepherds

The growing discontent you see globally is the natural, spiritual weariness that settles upon people when they realize they are being led by wolves masquerading as shepherds. They are driven by an aggressive, self-serving ambition that was clearly foretold in Scripture as a sign of the last days:

> *But understand this, that in the last days there will come times of difficulty. For people will be* ***lovers of self****, lovers of money, boastful, proud, abusive, disobedient to their parents, ungrateful, unholy, heartless, unappeasable, slanderous, without self-control, brutal, not loving good, treacherous, reckless, swollen with conceit,* ***lovers of pleasure rather than lovers of God****, having the*

> *appearance of godliness, but denying its power. Avoid such people.*
>
> —2 Timothy 3:1–5 ESV (emphasis added)

This passage perfectly describes the character of the leaders of today—those who demand allegiance not through moral authority or service, but through manipulation, ego, and the promise of worldly pleasure. They are content to see the world burn in division, so long as they remain on top.

The Winter of Our Discontent

The opening soliloquy of Shakespeare's *Richard III* includes this remarkable prose: "Now is the winter of our discontent Made glorious summer by this sun of York; And all the clouds that lour'd upon our house in the deep bosom of the ocean buried."[7] Taken in its intended context, the orator is celebrating the bright future ahead as they pass from despair into the glorious summer of a new era.

Unfortunately, our world is marching in lockstep toward our winter of discontent and desolation. Pulitzer Prize-winning author, John Steinbeck, set forth his own elucidated rendition of man's inner struggles in the aptly titled novel *The Winter of Our Discontent.* Through Steinbeck's protagonist,

---

[7] William Shakespeare, *Richard III*, ed. David Bevington (Bantam Books, 1988), 1.1.1.

Ethan Allen Hawley, we peer through the eyes of one man as he struggles through setbacks and tragedy, eventually embracing every immoral concession, to reimagine a niche of narcissistic personage.

Steinbeck wrote, "In business and in politics a man must carve and maul his way through men to get to be King of the mountain."[8] I draw reference to Steinbeck's Hawley as the example of modern-day politicians and challenge you with this query: Do the ends justify the means? Dissatisfaction with circumstances befallen our "hero" allows discontent to evolve into a caustic coalescence of envy and entitlement resulting in a moral betrayal of self-justified profit over societal jurisprudence. Suffice it to say I challenge anyone to contradict the assertion that our failed society at large is the result of our collective malaise toward those who have traded moral value for their rapacious remunerations. Have we not watched the world crumble as nations struggle to find leadership and self-serving demagogues manipulate their citizenry to achieve their evil outcomes? The winter of our discontent is now upon us.

As I reflect on *The Winter of Our Discontent*, it is almost as if Steinbeck were peering through a glass darkly upon our world today as his protagonist declares: "Strength and

---

[8] John Steinbeck, *The Winter of Our Discontent* (Penguin Books, 2008), 149.

success—they are above morality, above criticism."[9] Societal norms have become a win-at-all-cost objective that places desired outcomes above any moral standard or rule of law. Blind faith in supporting a platform of liberal progressivism has unleashed a set of ideals furthered through equivocation and lacking in detail. Progressive politicians attempt to captivate the public with grandiose visions often dominated by "all-or-nothing" mandates with promises of universal healthcare, total renewable energy transformations within a single decade, and radical economic overhauls of housing markets and employment models. These proposals function as brilliant stagecraft, designed to stir emotion and signal moral superiority. Yet, beneath the towering rhetoric, the structural reality is intentionally obscured. The precise costs, logistical requirements, and inevitable sacrifices are kept in the shadows, hidden behind the glare of the spotlight. Above all, claims are both grandiose and ambiguous, which is why the leftist cognoscenti avoid debate as if they haven't the time to waste on trivialities, preferring to hide behind their ever-present cloak of identity politics. Anyone who speaks out against socialist/communist ideals is declared a fascist or worse. The vagueness of proposals like the "Green New Deal" is not an oversight; it is a tactical necessity of the political theater. To provide specifics would be to invite accountability, and in a system built on image, accounta-

---

[9] Steinbeck, *The Winter of Our Discontent*, 175.

bility is a liability. This would seem to confirm beyond any reasonable doubt that, for our current-day provocateurs, the ends justify the means.

Of course, such Machiavellian tactics are nothing new and to ascribe them to one side only would be to mislead ourselves, and in so doing, become guilty of that which we despise. Ah, but therein lies the entry point to this endeavor of wills. Those with the dirtiest hands often cast aspersions with the loudest voice. Politics can be a subterfuge of lies with the guilty projecting upon other persons or groups the very misdeeds in which they are immersed up to their necks.

The Eternal Pursuit Versus the Finite World

Maybe it is time to take a step back, look at our world and ask the question: What prize are we hoping to win? We are distracted by the pettiness of our politicians while we lose sight of the larger world around us falling into chaos. That's not to say we shouldn't engage in our elections as we should always make our voices heard and participate in the voting process. But don't allow a finite worldview to replace the more important eternal pursuits that believers in Christ must strive to attain. Remember this question posed by Jesus: "*For what shall it profit a man, if he shall gain the whole world, and lose his own soul*" (Mark 8:36)?

When one subscribes to a limited worldview, it can be easy to forget that our battles are not to be waged man against man. But believers are to adhere to these words from the Apostle Paul:

> *For we do not wrestle against flesh and blood, but against the rulers, against the authorities, against the cosmic powers over this present darkness, against the spiritual forces of evil in the heavenly places. Therefore, take up the whole armor of God, that you may be able to withstand in the evil day, and having done all, to stand firm. Stand therefore, having fastened on the belt of truth, and having put on the breastplate of righteousness, and, as shoes for your feet, having put on the readiness given by the gospel of peace. In all circumstances take up the shield of faith, with which you can extinguish all the flaming darts of the evil one; and take the helmet of salvation, and the sword of the Spirit, which is the word of God, praying at all times in the Spirit, with all prayer and supplication. To that end, keep alert with all perseverance, making supplication for all the saints.*
>
> —Ephesians 6:12–18 ESV

What we see today is "*this present darkness*" to which Paul was referring, the spiritual forces of evil, revealing themselves through the manipulations of our world. The books of Ezekiel and Revelation describe a leader, Gog, and the land of Magog, rising in battle against Israel. These are described as end-times prophecies of what will be. It would take days to explain the interpretations by many theologians, but suffice it to say, most all conclude that the land of Magog represents portions of current day Russia, Iran, Turkey, and other Eastern Bloc nations that will join against a common enemy.

As the war between Russia and Ukraine continues, we see Russian, Iranian, and North Korean troops—with support from China and Turkey—working side-by-side in this conflict. This unholy alliance is staggering when you consider the eschatology of the Bible. In fact, in July 2022, a summit was convened in Tehran that included Putin, Erdogan, and the leaders of Iran in a blatant anti-American alliance that includes Iran's terrorist proxies such as Hezbollah.

True believers in Christ must keep in mind that we are called to be salt and light in an ever-darkening world. We must understand that so many around us do not know the truth of the gospel and if we don't share the good news of salvation, who will? The attacks on our morals, beliefs, and our nation's foundations are painful and hurtful, but we must arm ourselves with the truth and stand firmly on God's principles. We should participate eagerly in our civic duties and vote in support of candidates and resolutions that support our godly principles, but we should also strive to avoid labeling those who oppose our values as our enemies. All have been created by God, in His own image, and those that reject Him are given over to their own evil ways. They are unable to decipher truth from lies and thus fall under the spell of evil cast by the father of lies.

Jesus offered these words of hope and instruction when asked by his disciples about the end times and his own return:

As Jesus was sitting on the Mount of Olives, the disciples came to him privately. "Tell us," they said, "when will this happen, and what will be the sign of your coming and of the end of the age?"

Jesus answered: "Watch out that no one deceives you. For many will come in my name, claiming, 'I am the Messiah,' and will deceive many. You will hear of wars and rumors of wars but see to it that you are not alarmed. Such things must happen, but the end is still to come. Nation will rise against nation, and kingdom against kingdom. There will be famines and earthquakes in various places. All these are the beginning of birth pains.

"Then you will be handed over to be persecuted and put to death, and you will be hated by all nations because of me. At that time many will turn away from the faith and will betray and hate each other, and many false prophets will appear and deceive many people. Because of the increase of wickedness, the love of most will grow cold, but the one who stands firm to the end will be saved. ***And this gospel of the kingdom will be preached in the whole world as a testimony to all nations, and then the end will come.****"*

—Matthew 24:3–14 NIV (emphasis added)

We no longer live in an era when evil feels the need to hide in the shadows. Progressive leadership offers the state as a hollow replacement for God. These architects of a "new morality" have stolen the high ground, using it as a platform to project their own transgressions onto their foes while stoking the fires of division with dangerous rhetoric. They operate on the dark conviction that their ends justify any means—even if that requires dismantling truth itself.

As we find ourselves in our own deep winter of discontent, we are forced to confront a reality we can no longer ignore: Can we sit idly by while our world collapses under the weight of this deception? We would do well to consider this sobering observation by Hawley, Steinbeck's protagonist: "Intention, good or bad, is not enough. There's an awful lot of inactive kindness which is nothing but laziness, not wanting any trouble, confusion, or effort."[10]

The time for "inactive kindness" has passed. If we believe in a foundational truth—a bedrock that does not shift with the political winds—we must decide where we stand. Are you simply going along to fit in, fearing the discomfort of the spotlight? Do you truly know what you believe? In a world of performance and projection, the only response to the theater of lies is a life anchored in the immovable truth of Christ.

[10] Steinbeck, *The Winter of Our Discontent*, 264.

Seven:

THE RECKONING: THE MIRROR, THE STUMBLING BLOCK, AND THE CHURCH

Woe unto them that call evil good, and good evil; that put darkness for light, and light for darkness; that put bitter for sweet and sweet for bitter!

—Isaiah 5:20

In the previous chapters, we peeled back the layers of global chaos, identifying the prophetic Great Divide, the rise of lawlessness, and the Machiavellian tactics of leaders who thrive on manufactured discontent. It is easy, in this environment, to become an observer, pointing fingers at the "them" who are causing the ruin. It is far harder to turn the lens inward and ask the most difficult question: Am I contributing to the division, and is my spiritual house in order?

The spiritual battle Paul describes in Ephesians 6:12 is against cosmic powers, not "*flesh and blood.*" If we truly believe this, our immediate focus must shift from political condemnation to personal and corporate spiritual integrity.

Looking in the Mirror: The Danger of Self-Perception and Pride

To truly understand our place in this world, we must step outside the comfort of our own perceptions and conduct a fearless inventory of the heart. Most of us are quick to categorize the world into the good, the bad, and the ugly—often conveniently placing ourselves in the light while casting our "foes" in the dark. Yet, we must confront the sobering reality of our own moral compromises. We must look closely to see if we have begun to substitute darkness for light and bitter for sweet, or if we have fallen into the trap of calling evil good simply because it serves our narrative.

True goodness is not defined by our proximity to a political tribe or the height of our rhetoric; it is found in our alignment with an unchanging truth. Without conducting an honest self-assessment, we risk becoming the very thing we claim to despise: a soul lost in the gray area where convenience has replaced conviction.

We need to be careful in how we perceive ourselves versus others; pride has a way of creeping in, and we must guard our hearts and minds. Otherwise, we can easily fall into a trap set by the enemy. Believers are not immune to pride and other failures in character and morality. Satan, our true adversary, experienced his great fall due to pride and the love of self over the love of God.

The winter of discontent that plagues our culture germinates from seed in the human heart. Before we can effectively stand against the forces of darkness, we must honestly assess our own spiritual state. The world preaches a "win-at-all-cost" mentality, but for the believer, that pursuit must stop where humility begins.

We are called to be salt and light; yet, we often serve up judgment and self-righteousness. It is essential to recognize the difference between boldly proclaiming God's uncompromised truth and simply condemning those who disagree with our cultural or political views. The latter is noise; the former is the gospel.

Consider Jesus's challenge to each of us in Matthew 7:3: "*And why beholdest thou the mote that is in thy brother's eye, but considerest not the beam that is in thine own eye*?" This passage remains a constant, painful spiritual plumb line. When we engage in endless, petty political squabbles and allow ourselves to be consumed by anger, bitterness, and vengeance (the very hallmarks of the father of lies we identified in chapter 5), we compromise our ability to shine the light of Christ. We become part of the problem, trading the eternal pursuit for the finite victory of being "right" on social media or in public discourse.

Anger, bitterness, and hatred are everywhere these days in our culture and permeating every aspect of our lives. Journalism, as it was intended to be, is dead, replaced with agenda-driven opinions that masquerade as fact-based news. The world is being overcome by the dark evil spirit of lies and vengeance, the hallmarks of the father of lies, that allow no place for debate; you either agree with the mainstream narrative or become the target of the oppressive voice that controls media, entertainment, and the news. Justice is not balanced; up is down; right is wrong. We are not to question the worldly agenda unless we are willing to pay a heavy toll. The Bible warns, "*Woe unto them that call evil good, and good evil, who put darkness for light, and light for darkness, who put bitter for sweet, and sweet for bitter*" (Isaiah 5:20)!

An honest self-assessment must confront this question: Has the chaos of the world successfully stolen my peace and replaced my love with contempt? If we are to be true witnesses, our demeanor, our words, and our integrity must starkly contrast with the corrupt, gaslighting nature of worldly leadership.

The Stumbling Block: Our Perception of Others

The second crucial step in navigating this chaotic age is redefining how we view the people around us, especially those who vehemently oppose our biblical worldview. It is impossible to effectively reach someone for Christ if we have first judged and condemned them in our hearts.

The Bible makes a clear distinction: We are to discern evil ideology and sin, but we must never condemn a person who is created in God's image. When we label a person as an enemy simply because they have been given over to their own evil ways (as Romans 1 describes), we forget that we, too, were once slaves to sin.

It is not our responsibility to punish the unregenerate for acting unregenerate; instead, we are to offer them the way out. Our battle is not against the "*flesh and blood*" they represent, but against the "*cosmic powers*" that manipulate them. If we fight the person, we play the enemy's game. If we pray for and witness to the person, we engage in the true spiritual war.

This perspective is crucial to the Great Commission. If we believe the end is drawing near, we must treat every encounter as an urgent, final opportunity to share the gospel. Our focus cannot be on correcting every political or moral misstep of the lost; it must be on offering the redemption that only comes through Christ's sacrifice. Love, not judgment, opens the door to that conversation.

The Crisis of the Pulpit: Denying the Cross for the Crown

This brings us to the question of the collective body of believers: Is the Church serving the needs of society or serving itself? We see deception in the world, but don't be fooled, deception has also found its way into the church. The pulpit in many modern-day sanctuaries is no longer a platform of truth that challenges the faithful to adhere to the high calling of our Lord. It has become an arbiter of feelings, a pacifier of emotional reactions aimed at soothing and comforting congregations that have lost their way. "Feel-good" theology has no place in truth; in practice, it waters down and, in many cases, ignores the Word of God, leading more people down the broad path toward destruction.

Why should it matter if a church wants people to feel better about themselves? I'll tell you why it matters. When truth is replaced with feelings and emotions, you will lose your way and be left to find your own way out of darkness. Truth is light; our world is darkness. Without truth, you become blind in a darkened world.

Prosperity faith, feel-good doctrines, and self-empowerment are not aligned with the message of Jesus Christ. Pantheism always points inward to create a belief that all power and spiritualism are attained within your own being—that you can rise to the level of a god. Consider these words from a prominent purveyor of this theology, Joel Osteen:

> Every setback means you're one step closer to seeing the dream come to pass. Indeed, it is as important to learn how to receive a blessing as it is to be willing to give one. Don't just accept whatever comes your way in life. You were born to win; you were born

> for greatness; you were created to be a champion in life.[11]

On the surface, these words may seem to be uplifting, but in a spiritual context, they are dangerous and full of deceit. They don't prepare believers in Christ for the coming persecution they will face. If you think the Christian journey is primarily about feeling better about yourself or your situation in life, you're on the wrong path.

Notice that Jesus didn't tell his followers that they were champions in life and that every setback meant they were one step closer to success. Listen to what Jesus teaches us:

> *Blessed are they which are persecuted for righteousness' sake: for theirs is the kingdom of heaven. Blessed are ye, when men shall revile you, and persecute you, and shall say all manner of evil against you falsely, for my sake. Rejoice, and be exceedingly glad: for great is your reward in heaven: for so persecuted they the prophets which were before you.*
>
> —Matthew 5:10–12

Rejoice and be exceedingly glad when we are persecuted? That doesn't seem to mesh with the "born to win" narrative. You can't reconcile a message that says it's all about

---

[11] Joel Osteen, *I Declare: 31 Promises to Speak Over Your Life* (FaithWords, 2012), 34.

you—your success, your own personal happiness—with the message from Jesus about putting ourselves second, and denying ourselves, so that we can follow Him. You must choose; you can't have it both ways.

When the Church focuses on its own programs, comfort, and financial stability, seeking to avoid the cross and claim the crown early, it fails the society it is called to serve. The Church is meant to be the hospital for the spiritually sick and the lighthouse for a world drowning in darkness, but a church focused on self-preservation is a lamp hidden under a bushel; it is useless to the world and an offense to God.

> *But know this: Hard times will come in the last days. For people will be lovers of self, lovers of money, boastful, proud, demeaning, disobedient to parents, ungrateful, unholy, unloving, irreconcilable, slanderers, without self-control, brutal, without love for what is good, traitors, reckless, conceited, lovers of pleasure rather than lovers of God,* ***holding to the form of godliness but denying its power. Avoid these people****.*
>
> —2 Timothy 3:1–5 CSB (emphasis added)

If the gospel of the kingdom will be preached in the whole world as a testimony to all nations, and then the end will come (Matthew 24:14), the Church has one, nonnegotiable mission: to proclaim the truth. We are called to action, and our purpose is to be that light in a dark world.

Stand at the ready, put love above hate, focus not on

yourself, and focus on Jesus. Then your own troubles will be kept in their proper perspective. Our trials are temporary; our destination is eternal. Live in the hope that comes with the resurrection; we are redeemed with God. Comparing ourselves to others is a meaningless pursuit that only leads to exhaustion. Scripture humbles us with the truth that our own works are like "filthy rags," yet it encourages us with the greater truth: In Christ, God no longer sees our flaws. He sees us as spotless, cherished, and complete.

Eight:

THE TRAGEDY OF THE HIDDEN LAMPSTAND: THE COMPLACENT CHURCH

> *We have become so comfortable and complacent in the way we do church that we don't want any outsiders to mess it up.*

The world is spiraling into the darkness foretold by prophecy—a darkness characterized by lawlessness, hatred, and the rise of leaders consumed by the love of self. In this final, urgent hour, the Church, the singular body empowered by the Holy Spirit to be the light of the world, finds itself at a tragic crossroads. Rather than standing boldly as the "*city set on a hill*" (Matthew 5:14), too many modern congregations resemble a lamp hidden under a bushel—a comfortable, self-referential club that has lost both its flavor and its urgency.

In the previous chapter, we exposed the dangers of the crisis of the pulpit, where the challenging call of the cross is traded for the soothing promise of a self-empowerment gospel. This compromise has a profound and paralyzing consequence: complacency.

The Culture of Comfort and the Lost Calling

Church in America is comfortable, consistent, pre-planned, and delivered in a tidy package each week to the faithful. Deviate from that organized delivery model and church leaders will hear about it in no uncertain terms. Regular complaints include temperature (too hot or cold), music (too loud or too contemporary), and of course, the pastor went too long with his sermon. Overall, these are not seen as problematic; they're sort of the usual stuff. But they are symptoms of a deeper contagion. Somewhere along the way, we seem to have lost our true calling and, as a result, the way we "do church" has become more of an entertainment and social gathering. Too many churches are no longer missional in their purpose; they have vacated their duty to serve and provide for those in our communities.

The Numbers Don't Lie: A Crisis of Attendance

We can analyze the health of our churches through two standards: attendance and spiritual well-being. While spiritual well-being is not something that can be measured, attendance certainly is, and the numbers do not paint a positive picture.

According to a 2017 Gallup telephone survey, 40 percent of Americans reported attending a church service in the previous seven days, which would total nearly 130 million people. However, more in-depth research conducted by the Evangelical Covenant Church, which took data from over 200,000 orthodox Christian churches over a ten-year span, found the actual number of people in a pew each Sunday in America is closer to 52 million—a staggering difference. This number indicates that only 17 percent of America goes to church each week. Numbers don't tell the whole story, but they do not speak well of the spiritual well-being of our congregations or for the Church's outreach efforts.

Losing the Salt: The Failure of Distinction

Jesus used two powerful metaphors to describe the believer's role in the world: salt and light. Salt, in ancient times, served two primary purposes: preservation and flavor. When a church becomes complacent, focused entirely on the comfort and entertainment of its attendees, it loses its preserving power.

We have become so comfortable and complacent with the way we do church that we don't want any outsiders to mess it up. In other words, we will fight for the precise worship style or carpet color we want, but we will yawn at the thought of our neighbors going to hell.

When the church embraces its own sovereign space, celebrating within the comfortable confines of its own creation, surrounded by a like-minded social circle, they stop reaching out, instead choosing to focus inwards. Isolated inside this bunker of truth, they lose sight of their one true calling-to share the love of Jesus with a lost world.

The Attractional Trap: Misguided Priorities

The Great Commission is the one true calling that speaks to all Christians; it was given by Jesus Christ in Matthew 28: "*Go and make disciples of all nations.*" Period. That is our calling.

But we have confused attraction with outreach. As Thom Rainer said, "We became so enamored with the worship service we concluded that it was our outreach. But cool and dynamic worship services are not outreach into our communities. They are attractions to attend."[12] It is similar to a church that thinks its prime location equates to outreach,

---

[12] Thom Rainer, *Why American Churches Are at a Tipping Point* (Lifeway Research, 2019), 1.

relying on the premise of the movie *Field of Dreams* with its catchphrase, "If you build it, they will come." If that were the case, how do you explain the 83 percent of Americans who sleep in every Sunday morning?

We stand firm, often as the only voice, to protect the unborn child. We should look inward, with that same urgency, and demand of ourselves that we stand up and speak out about our Savior, Jesus, denying him before no man and sharing the love that He has for everyone. If our church leadership is not calling us to witness to our neighbors, coworkers, and those that cross our paths each day, then we should ask why.

We need to take a step back and look at our priorities. What if we fought for lost souls just as hard as we fought for the unborn child? What if we trusted in Jesus and believed in our hearts that He truly is the miracle worker, then set our priorities toward salvation first? Salvation is the cornerstone upon which we can rebuild our society.

Denny Burk, professor of biblical studies at Boyce College, recently shared this regarding the ministry of Joel Osteen: "The prosperity gospel that Osteen preaches will damn the very people he intends to help (if they believe it), and he appears completely unaware of the darkness into which he plunges his followers."[13] This runs in direct opposition to the teachings of Christ as shared earlier from

---

[13] Denny Burk, "Joel Osteen's Christianity Without a Cross," *Christianity News* (October 15, 2007), 2.

Matthew 16. There is nothing wrong with being happy, but in the context of Christian faith, we find true happiness through dedication and perseverance in Christ, not in worldly possessions or by putting ourselves first.

The Warning of Laodicea and the Narrow Gate

The starkest warning against spiritual complacency comes from the Book of Revelation, aimed directly at the Church of Laodicea:

> *I know thy works, that thou art neither cold nor hot. I would thou wert cold or hot. So then because thou art lukewarm, and neither cold nor hot, I will spue thee out of my mouth. Because thou sayest, I am rich, and increased with goods, and have need of nothing; and knowest not that thou art wretched, and miserable, and poor, and blind, and naked.*
>
> —Revelation 3:15–17

This passage perfectly mirrors the danger facing the modern complacent church. In seeking to avoid offense, difficulty, and persecution, we risk becoming useless to the Lord, causing Him to reject us as lukewarm. The road to life is intentionally difficult:

> *Enter through the narrow gate. For wide is the gate and broad is the road that leads to destruction, and many*

> *enter through it. But small is the gate and narrow the road that leads to life, and only a few find it.*
>
> —Matthew 7:13–14 NIV

To the faithful, I ask: Are you evangelizing according to our shared calling from Jesus? If you truly believe that you have been saved through grace and that Jesus Christ died for all sinners, then step up and share that message! The world is lost, and we are the light, but if we hide that light under a bushel then what good are we?

The time for complacency is over. The days are dark, and the harvest is ready. The world does not need another social club; it desperately needs the uncompromised light, the preserving salt, and the courageous urgency of a Church that is prepared to take up its cross and preach the kingdom. The time for the Church to assume its prophetic role is now.

Nine:

THE POISON OF PROSPERITY: THE FALSE GOSPEL OF THE PROSPERITY MESSAGE

For the time will come when people will not tolerate sound doctrine, but according to their own desires, will multiply teachers for themselves because they have an itch to hear what they want to hear.

—2 Timothy 4:3 CSB

The complacency and self-focus that have crippled the American Church did not happen by accident; they were intentionally nurtured by a false, seductive theology that promises comfort without the cross. We have briefly touched on the dangers of feel-good preaching, but the prosperity gospel, the message of "best self" Christianity, is so pervasive, so toxic, and so effective at drawing crowds while discipling no one, that it demands a full, uncompromising exposure. It is the ultimate expression of Laodicean self-sufficiency—a deceptive doctrine that has hijacked the mission of the Church. "*Beloved, believe not every spirit, but try the spirits whether they are of God, because many false prophets have gone out into the world* (1 John 4:1).

The old axiom holds true in the spiritual realm more than any other: If it's too good to be true, it most likely is false. This warning applies directly to doctrines that promise health and wealth for a minimal investment of faith or cash, words that tickle our ears or play on our vulnerabilities.

Success That Fails: Attraction Without Conversion

The greatest danger to the Church's mission today is the counterfeit message of "feel-good evangelism" or the prosperity faith. This message is successful at drawing massive crowds but utterly fails at discipling converts, replacing biblical truth with consumer-friendly affirmations.

When I critique this doctrine, I often face resistance, with proponents pointing to the sheer size of ministries that preach this message. I once engaged in a conversation with someone who used a very popular megachurch in the Houston area as an example of a thriving ministry, citing its massive crowds and television audience. My reply remains firm: If that's the best example you have, you just helped make my case that the Church in America is dying.

This style of ministry and many others like it largely avoid talk of sin, consequence, or the necessity of self-denial, focusing instead on personal happiness and worldly success. The core deception lies in the simple omission of essential biblical truths.

Deceptive Roots: Hill, Roberts, and the Word of Faith

The thriving prosperity message is often labeled the Word of Faith movement, which traces its philosophical roots not to Scripture, but to the writings of Napoleon Hill and his book *Think and Grow Rich* published in 1937. Hill wrote of his imaginary "cabinet of Invisible Counselors" made up of great minds that would meet with him each night to discuss ways to improve his character and build his thoughts and ideas. He confessed that this practice, which began in his imagination around a boardroom table, over time became so real he often feared the realism and what it meant. Hill would later describe how these "invisible counselors" had guided him through crises to ultimate wealth and power.

The very description of his influences from these beings, which he would later describe as "talismans," goes against biblical warnings:

> *There shall not be found among you anyone who burns his son or his daughter as an offering, anyone who practices divination or tells fortunes or interprets omens, or a sorcerer or a charmer or a medium or a necromancer or one who inquires of the dead, for whoever does these things is an abomination to the Lord.*
>
> —Deuteronomy 18:10–12 ESV

Such dealings open the door to demonic influence and the works of Satan in our lives. The fact that Hill would use the term *talismans* is quite telling, as the term itself attributes mystical powers upon an object. A reasonable mind must ask, what exactly were the "talismans" that guided and inspired Hill if not demons?

In the early 1950s, a young evangelist from Tulsa, Oklahoma, named Oral Roberts, began a ministry of prosperity preaching through the giving of "seed faith" money. The foundation of his beliefs was attributed, in part, to none other than Napoleon Hill. Roberts's ministry grew exponentially as he spread the word of prosperity, namely that by giving to his ministry, God would return that investment in riches beyond belief. As his empire grew, it influenced others to do the same, which is why Oral Roberts is often referred to as the father of the prosperity gospel. He is cited as the major influence, directly or indirectly, of Kenneth Hagin, Kenneth Copeland, and Fred Price. From these three, specifically Hagin and his Rhema Bible Training Center, we have generations of prosperity ministries founded in the "name it and claim it" genre.

Regardless of the minister, we have a responsibility as believers to test the doctrine that is given out, using the infallible word of God to ensure that their teaching holds up to the truth. The Apostle Paul warned of this specific deception—a time when people would actively seek out preachers who catered to their desire for comfort as we previously noted from 2 Timothy 4:3. This passage perfectly describes the demand for a gospel that soothes the ego while ignoring the soul. Preachers who focus on "how to be your best self" and "how to be happy in life" are simply meeting the market demand described by Paul, offering a message that avoids sound instruction by the Word of God, yet is palatable to the masses.

The Seed Is the Word, Not Money: Exposing the "Seed Faith" Lie

The prosperity message is very loosely based upon the parable of the Sower from Matthew 13, where Jesus tells of sowing seed and states that the seed, which fell on fertile soil was returned to the sower one hundredfold. Ministries that preach "seed faith" money cherry-pick these few verses and then define the "seed" as money invested in the church, making it sound very appealing to those in need to think that if you give ten dollars you will be rewarded by God with one thousand dollars.

This is a deliberate and dangerous use of Scripture out of context. To expose this fallacy, simply read the entire thirteenth chapter of Matthew, and you will see that Jesus further clarifies the seed referenced is the Word of God, not money or other valuables.

The danger of these types of messages is that they reduce God to being closer to our own level, whereby we develop a twisted *quid pro quo*, a contract with God, which requires that He provide a specific material value for that which you have given. To even consider that God is to be bargained with and held to our own exacting standards is not only dangerous but runs close to blasphemy.

The Cross Versus Mammon: Jesus's Litmus Test on Wealth

The first place to go when examining any doctrine is to the example given to us by Jesus Christ Himself, demonstrating the fundamentals of a life lived in direct obedience to our heavenly Father. Would Jesus support a doctrine that specifically guides followers to a path of personal gain and greater wealth?

In Matthew 19, we have the example of the rich young ruler. After the young man claimed he had kept all the commandments, Jesus gave him one final instruction: Go and sell all that he owned and give it to the poor. The young ruler walked away in anguish. Jesus used this single command as a litmus test to expose the young man's fallacy: He had made his wealth the focus of his worship and, through his own greed, was not following the commandment to love his neighbor as himself.

In relating this to prosperity, Jesus showed how dangerous greed and the love of money can be, diverting our faithfulness to worldly possessions. One does not go hand in hand with the other; they are contradictory in nature. Jesus instructs us:

> *Do not lay up for yourselves treasures on earth, where moth and rust destroy and where thieves break in and steal; but lay up for yourselves treasures in heaven, where neither moth nor rust destroys and where thieves do not break in and steal. For where your treasure is, there your heart will be also.*
>
> —Matthew 6:19–21 ESV

Jesus warns that where your treasure is, there your heart will be also. He continues by saying:

> *No one can serve two masters. Either you will hate the one and love the other, or you will be devoted to the one and despise the other. You cannot serve God and money.*
>
> —Matthew 6:24 NIV

Jesus lived the life of a servant, saying in Matthew 20:28, *"Even as the Son of Man came not to be served, but to serve, and to give his life as a ransom for many"* (ESV). We are to strive to be Christlike in all our ways. Being obedient to God, serving those in need while placing their interest above your own, and focusing firmly on our Savior are the keys to having a more abundant life.

Heed the warnings of the Scriptures regarding false teachers, test the spirits, and ensure you are standing on firm doctrine according to the will of God. The greatest deception is one that promises everything the flesh desires, while quietly leading you down the broad path to destruction.

Ten:

THE INCONVENIENT TRUTH: WHY DO BAD THINGS HAPPEN TO GOOD PEOPLE?

As it is written, There is none righteous, no, not one; There is none that understandeth, There is none that seeketh after God. They are all gone out of the way, they are together become unprofitable; There is none that doeth good, no, not one.

—Romans 3:10–12

The prosperity gospel attempts to provide a neat, marketable answer to one of humanity's most persistent and painful questions: Why do bad things happen to good people?

The false preachers assert that suffering is either a punishment for insufficient faith, a lack of "seed money" or a failure to speak the right confession. But this man-centered theology collapses immediately when confronted with the crushing reality of global suffering, persecution, and terminal illness, often endured by the most devout and righteous among us. It is not inherently wrong to ask why bad things happen to good people, but the question contains a fundamental, flawed premise that must be corrected before we can seek a biblical answer.

Spiritual Blindness and the Flawed Premise

For the nonbeliever or the atheist, events such as devastating hurricanes, wildfires, or disease are often used to justify their nonbelief, becoming a point of debate that questions the very existence of a loving God. They conclude that if God is love, He should be all-protecting, a comic-book superhero averting disaster at every turn.

This misunderstanding stems from a lack of spiritual discernment. Natural man, not having come to a place of salvation, does not know God and therefore cannot understand the workings of our Creator in this world.

> *But the natural man receiveth not the things of the Spirit of God: for they are foolishness unto him: neither can he know them, because they are spiritually discerned.*
>
> —1 Corinthians 2:14

It is no wonder that men of great worldly knowledge are unable to make sense of the wisdom of God through His Word. Without the Holy Spirit to discern the Word, it is foolishness to the mind of man. They have no knowledge of Satan, the adversary who roams this earth searching for those they may devour (1 Peter 5:8). Consequently, they deduce that God does not exist, when in reality, they simply do not have the spiritual tools to understand the complexity of a world permeated by evil and sin.

Deconstructing the Term Good People

Even believers struggle with understanding the concept of "good people" in a fallen world. We often define a good person as someone who is law-abiding, a kind neighbor, or someone who gives to charity. These are worthy attributes, but they are measured against the low bar of human behavior, not the infinite standard of God's absolute holiness.

When we think of ourselves as "good," as if our works elevate us to a higher level of existence, we are on a slippery slope that can lead to a fall. The only good person, without fault, to ever walk the earth was Jesus Christ. We must weigh our self-assessment in the light of God's uncompromising standard:

> *As it is written, there is none righteous, no, not one: there is none who understandeth, there is none that*

> *seeketh after God. They are all gone out of the way, they are together become unprofitable; **there is none that doeth good, no, not one**.*
>
> —Romans 3:10–12 (emphasis added)

The Apostle Paul makes the comprehensive verdict undeniable: "*for **all have sinned** and fall short of the glory of God*" (Romans 3:23 emphasis added). Our best attempts at human goodness are worthless in God's sight: "*But we are all as an unclean thing, and all our righteousnesses are as filthy rags; and we all do fade as a leaf; and our iniquities, like the wind, have taken us away*" (Isaiah 64:6 emphasis added). In truth, there are no "good people" to whom bad things happen; there are only fallen people living in a fallen world.

The Source and Nature of Suffering

When a believer suffers, it is often a spiritual attack from the enemy, a consequence of the Fall or a refining process from the Lord, but it is **never** arbitrary.

1. **Suffering Is a Consequence of the Fall, Not Punishment:** When Adam and Eve chose self-will over God's command, sin entered the world (Romans 5:12), and the entire creation was cursed (Romans 8:20–22). This means that disease, natural disasters, and the pain of a paper cut

are all consequences of living in a world under the curse of sin. Suffering is the natural state of a fallen world.

A natural phenomenon, such as a hurricane or wildfire, does not mean a specific area on this earth is being punished. It is a circumstance that comes with living in this turbulent, corrupt world. "*For he maketh his sun to rise on the evil and on the good, and sendeth rain on the just and on the unjust*" (Matthew 5:45).

God allows the consequences of a broken world to affect everyone, regardless of their belief or moral standing. It is during these crises that believers have an opportunity to shine the light of Jesus Christ in their response, to grow in their own faith while sharing and helping others.

2. **Suffering Is a Refiner's Fire:** God, in His infinite wisdom, uses suffering not to punish His children, but to perfect them. The biblical purpose of trials is always redemptive—to move us away from self-reliance (the core prosperity lie) and toward Christ-dependence.

   Not only that, but we rejoice in our sufferings, knowing that ***suffering produces endurance, and endurance produces character, and character produces hope****, and hope does not put us to shame,*

> *because God's love has been poured into our hearts through the Holy Spirit who has been given to us.*
>
> —Romans 5:3–5 ESV (emphasis added)

A life without trials is a life without the character that only endurance can forge. God is constantly at work in our lives, molding us, building our character, growing our faith, so that we may glorify Him.

3. **The Example of Job:** The book of Job provides the definitive answer to the question of suffering. Job's suffering was a spiritual battlefield permitted by God to silence Satan's accusation that Job only served God for the material blessings he received. Job's endurance proved that true faith seeks God's presence, not His gifts.

Persecution and Perseverance for the Believer

There is no declaration in the entirety of God's Word that life for those who believe in Jesus Christ will be easier. To the contrary, Jesus warns us that becoming His follower invites the world's antagonism:

> *If the world hates you, know that it has hated me before it hated you. If you were of the world, the world would*

love you as its own; but because you are not of the world, but I chose you out of the world, therefore the world hates you.

—John 15:18–19 ESV

We are told not to be surprised by our trials, but to see them as participation in Christ's own suffering, preparing us for eternal rewards:

Beloved, think it not strange concerning the fiery trial which is to try you, as though some strange thing happened unto you: but rejoice, inasmuch as ye are partakers of Christ's sufferings; that, when his glory shall be revealed, ye may be glad also with exceeding joy.

—1 Peter 4:12–13

God allows us to face challenges, knowing that He is working in our lives:

We are pressed on every side by troubles, but we are not crushed. We are perplexed, but not driven to despair. We are hunted down, but never abandoned by God. We get knocked down, but we are not destroyed. Through suffering, our bodies continue to share in the death of Jesus so that the life of Jesus may also be seen in our bodies.

—2 Corinthians 4:8–11 NLT

We are to fight the good fight and push forward to finish the race, keeping our eyes fixed upon the prize, just as Paul did:

> *For I am already being poured out as a drink offering, and the time of my departure has come. I have fought the good fight, I have finished the race, I have kept the faith. Henceforth there is laid up for me the crown of righteousness, which the Lord, the righteous judge, will award to me on that day.*
>
> —2 Timothy 4:6 CSB

And just as Stephen demonstrated the utmost compassion to those who stoned him to death in Acts 7, we are called to lean on the Lord, knowing that this life is only the beginning and that our true rewards are waiting on the other side.

Conclusion: A Worn-Out Question, a Timeless Answer

The world asks, "Why do bad things happen to good people?" The Bible answers in showing us that bad things happen to *all* people because sin is the master of this world. And for the believer, those "bad things" are redeemed by a sovereign God to produce eternal good.

If you are suffering, remember the cross. Christ, the only truly innocent and righteous man to ever live, suffered the most horrific "bad thing" imaginable—not because of His sin, but because of ours. Our suffering gives us a fleeting moment of connection to His ultimate sacrifice, purifying our faith and preparing us for eternal life where, finally, there will be no more pain or tears.

Eleven:

THE DIGITAL PRISON: NARCISSISM AND CANCEL CULTURE

The danger here is profound: A hyper-focus on self can warp the Christian mission from glorifying God to glorifying the person God saved.

In previous chapters, we examined the prophetic geopolitical shifts and the surge of iniquity that marks the last days. Much of this darkness is amplified and accelerated through the interconnected infrastructure of the internet, and specifically, through social media. These platforms, designed for connections, have become perfectly engineered tools for spiritual decay, fueling two of the most destructive forces in modern culture: self-worship and summary judgment.

For generations, our formative years—from the sidelines of youth sports to the halls of the corporate world—were defined by a "team-first" philosophy. We were taught that success depended on shared goals and prioritizing the common good over personal glory. Today's digital landscape has flipped that script, ushering in a "selfie culture" in which the individual reigns supreme, and we are conditioned to relentlessly broadcast the minutiae of our lives above all else. The spiritual state of the world today is precisely captured in Paul's description of the moral landscape of the last days:

> *But understand this, that in the last days there will come times of difficulty. For people will be* ***lovers of self****, lovers of money, proud, arrogant, abusive, disobedient to their parents, ungrateful, unholy, heartless, unappeasable, slanderous, without self-control, brutal, not loving good, treacherous, reckless, swollen with conceit,* ***lovers of pleasure rather than lovers of God****, having the appearance of godliness, but denying its power.*
>
> —2 Timothy 3:1–5 ESV (emphasis added)

The list begins with the core characteristic of our age, "lovers of self" (narcissism), followed by subsequent traits, including "slanderous" and "unappeasable," perfectly describing the spiritual mechanism behind cancel culture.

The Cult of Self: Engineered Narcissism

Social media platforms are not neutral tools; they are environments designed to cultivate and monetize attention. The "like" button, the validation metrics, and the constant urge to post, record, or share transform the user's identity into a perpetual performance. This environment feeds the sinful nature of narcissism in ways never before possible:

- **Identity as Brand:** The focus shifts from being a genuine, humble follower of Christ to performing a curated, flawless version of oneself. Life becomes content. Our value is measured not by our character but by our reach, engagement, and virality.
- **Addiction to Affirmation:** Every notification is a dopamine hit, momentarily filling the deep void that only God can permanently satisfy. The pursuit of external validation becomes an addiction, leading to endless comparison and spiritual exhaustion.
- **Loss of Humility:** The most valuable spiritual growth often happens in private through prayer, repentance, and quiet service. Social media compels us to document every act, turning ministry into a performance and humility into a competitive commodity.

> The danger here is profound: A hyper-focus on self can warp the Christian mission from glorifying God to glorifying the person God saved.

The "Look at Me" Portfolio and the Mosaic Tile

Social media encourages us to create our own life narrative and control it, sharing only the best of times and manipulating our image to the likeness we want the world to see. Reality is what we create, resulting in a narcissistic playground gone wild. The very lexicon of our generation now includes the "selfie," a term that represents the new norm of self-idolatry and the pervasive "look at me" portfolio.

To understand the spiritual danger, consider a mosaic tile. Close-up, you see the individual pieces, which are plain, imperfect, and isolated, but you miss the glorious image they form collectively. Likewise, when we focus our view solely inward, becoming consumed with our own issues and perceived shortcomings, we lose sight of those around us whom we are called to serve as disciples. We become hypersensitive to our own needs, placing them above all else, and fall out of step with God's purpose for our life.

This inward, self-serving impulse is the exact opposite of the blueprint laid out by Jesus Christ. The greatest narcissist of all time is Satan, so caught up in his own beauty and power that he turned on the Creator. It is no wonder he is using that very tool, self-worship, to bring down believers and nonbelievers alike. Jesus Christ came to this earth, God in the flesh, and in his own words made clear His purpose: "*For even the Son of Man did not come to be served, but to serve, and to give his life as a ransom for many*" (Mark 10:45 ESV).

Jesus put everything aside and became the servant of mankind. This example goes so much further than just putting oneself aside; it helps us realize the overall value and benefits of living for others. When we put down our own selfish interests, we gain a broader perspective and the ability to focus on the true value of life as God intended for us.

The Attitude of Christ Versus the Prosperity Gospel

In Philippians 2, Paul urged all believers to do nothing out of selfish ambition or empty pride, but in humility, we should consider others more important than ourselves. Paul followed this with the divine revelation of the attitude of Christ as he detailed how Jesus emptied Himself, taking the form of a servant, humbling Himself and becoming obedient to death.

The "me first" religion, which lifts up self-interests and self-gratification (often disguised in the modern prosperity message and the empowerment of self), is in direct contrast with the message shared by Christ. This doctrine preys on "itching ears" by offering a form of godliness that is pleasing to our own desires—a gospel without the conviction, self-denial, or service required to truly follow Jesus.

The litmus test for any doctrine must be its comparison with the teachings and example of Jesus. The real danger of the "look at me" society is how it contradicts our calling from Christ, creating a stronghold of self-worship that is even creeping into the church. When we follow our Savior's example, we look beyond the single tile of our own self-interests, and God reveals the wonderful mosaic we share in Jesus Christ.

The Modern Pharisees: The Malice of Cancel Culture

If narcissism is the worship of self, cancel culture is the punitive expression of that worship. It is a mob-driven mechanism of public shaming and destruction that embodies many of the spiritual dangers foretold in Scripture, primarily a lack of grace, forgiveness, and due process.

When objective truth is replaced by subjective group sentiment (as discussed in chapter 4), the collective becomes the ultimate judge and executioner. Cancel culture operates on the following unbiblical principles:

- **Immediate and Absolute Judgment:** It bypasses the Christian concept of restorative justice, forgiveness, and repentance. A person is judged not by their current character, but by an isolated, often historic, error. There is no path to redemption; the judgment is instantaneous and eternal, mirroring the spiritual lawlessness that Jesus warned would abound.

- **Self-Righteous Anger:** Participation in cancel culture provides a feeling of moral superiority, allowing the participant to feel "good" by condemning another. This is the spiritual sin of the modern Pharisee, focusing fiercely on the speck in a brother's eye while ignoring the plank in their own. It is anger expressed for the sake of feeling righteous, not for the sake of reconciliation or truth.
- **Slander and Unappeasable Rage:** The spiritual root of cancel culture is found in the "slanderous" and "unappeasable" nature of people in the last days. The tools of modern media allow for mass-slander to spread instantaneously, destroying reputations and careers with devastating speed and permanence.

The believer is called to a fundamentally different path, one that extends the grace we received and focuses on personal reconciliation and forgiveness, not public ruin.

The Call to Digital Discernment

How should the disciple of Christ navigate this digital environment? The answer is not total isolation, but radical self-control and discernment:

- **Guard Your Focus:** Use social media as a tool for limited, purposeful connection or ministry, not as a source of identity or worth. Practice digital fasting to remind your heart that your value is found only in Christ, not in your follower count.
- **Reclaim Your Humility:** Resist the urge to turn every good deed into a post. When you pray, pray in secret. When you give, do so quietly. Cultivate a life that is deep, not just wide.
- **Offer Grace, Reject the Mob:** Refuse to participate in the spiritual savagery of public shaming. When confronted with another person's offense, practice the model of Matthew 18 and go to them privately. If you must speak, let your words be seasoned with grace and aimed at restoration, not destruction.

Social media is a fleeting reflection of the deeper spiritual war. By denying the self-worship it demands and rejecting the malice of judgment it encourages, the believer can stand firm, keeping their eyes fixed on the eternal rewards, rather than the momentary, addictive applause of the world.

Twelve:

WHAT IS WRONG WITH THE WORLD?

The path to lawlessness begins not with ignorance, but with willful rejection and a failure to show gratitude.

In 1905, *The London Times* famously posed the question to G. K. Chesterton and other prominent writers: "What is wrong with the world?" Chesterton's immediate and iconic reply was simply: "Dear Sirs, I am."

His response remains a timeless truth: The world's problem is not external; it is internal. It is the sin and rebellion residing in the heart of every human being. For the believer seeking to discern the final signs of the age, this profound truth must be our starting point. The collapse of civil society, the rise of narcissism, and the acceleration of lawlessness are not random global trends; they are the predictable, inevitable consequences of a world that has collectively turned its back on the divine foundation of truth and has embraced the seductive whispers of the enemy.

The harsh reality is that nothing is wrong today that hasn't been wrong since Satan introduced sin into our world. As Ecclesiastes 1:9 states, "*The thing that hath been, it is that which shall be; and that which is done is that which shall be done: and there is no new thing under the sun.*" Every generation thinks its sins are innovative, yet we are only passing through a narrative that has been lived out countless times.

The proper question to ask today is: Why do we see *more* evil, immorality, despair, and hopelessness all around? The answer is the systematic removal of God from our society. We do not live in a vacuum; when you remove love, the void is immediately filled with hate. God is love in the purest form; Lucifer is hate. Look around you: The world we see today is a world that has refused God.

The Spiritual Diagnosis: The Great Falling Away

The world has removed God from the public eye—from schools, courtrooms, and civic spaces. In our 24-7 information age, evil and depravity are visible everywhere, resulting in the spiritual atmosphere, which the Apostle Paul describes in 2 Timothy chapter 3.

This is not merely a list of bad behavior; it is a spiritual diagnosis of malice. Every symptom stems from the core problem: self-worship. When God is dethroned, the self is installed as the ultimate authority, leading to the terrifying moral profile of godlessness in the last days (2 Timothy 3). The most disturbing warning for the discerning believer is those "*holding to the form of godliness but denying its power.*" This tells us the deception will often wear a religious mask, looking Christian, but lacking the Holy Spirit's power to convict sin or demand self-denial.

Satan's Master Strategy: The Blame Game

If the problem is the human heart, the influence that feeds this problem is Satan. The enemy's master strategy is not overt, recognizable evil, but deception. He runs a masterful endgame, using the nonstop news cycle to spew his vile hatred and deceit at every opportunity, causing the lost to fall into his traps.

Satan works to provoke the lost and the weak into vengeance, strife, and even murder. Then, the evil one whispers into the ears of the lost and believers alike and poses the question, "Why would a loving God allow such evil things?" Satan is guilty of all evil and should be held responsible, yet he is clever enough to hide behind his cloak of subterfuge as the world falls for his lies and turns their anger toward God. The world cries out for justice but then blames the just. Satan perpetrates his evil desires upon man and then convinces man to blame God.

The Result: Given Over to a Reprobate Mind

What happens when a person, or an entire civilization, persistently rejects the truth and the saving power of God? The consequence is a profound spiritual judgment where God simply allows humanity to reap what it has sown.

The Apostle Paul details the path to delusion in Romans chapter 1, showing the progression from revelation to rejection to consequence:

1. **The Clarity of Revelation**

   God has always revealed Himself clearly. People are without excuse because:

   Since what can be known about God is evident among them, because God has shown it to them. For his invisible attributes, that is, his eternal power and divine nature, have been clearly seen since the creation of the world, being understood through what he has made. ***As a result, people are without excuse*** (Romans 1:19–20 CSB emphasis added).

2. **The Exchange of Truth for a Lie**

   The path to lawlessness begins not with ignorance, but with willful rejection and a failure to show gratitude.

> *For though they knew God, they did not glorify him as God or show gratitude. Instead, their thinking became worthless, and their senseless hearts were darkened. Claiming to be wise, they became fools and exchanged the glory of the immortal God for images resembling mortal man, birds, four-footed animals, and reptiles. Therefore, God* ***delivered them over*** *in the desires of their hearts to sexual impurity, so that their bodies were degraded among themselves.* ***They exchanged the truth of God for a lie, and worshiped and served what has been created instead of the Creator****, who is praised forever. Amen* (Romans 1:21–25 CSB emphasis added).

This "giving over" is the terrifying spiritual judgment where God stops restraining humanity's desires. The final stage of this judgment is the reprobate mind:

> *And because they did not think it worthwhile to acknowledge God,* ***God delivered them over to a corrupt mind so that they do what is not right.*** *They are filled with all unrighteousness, evil, greed, and wickedness. They are full of envy, murder, quarrels, deceit, and malice. They are gossips, slanderers, God-haters, arrogant, proud, boastful, inventors of evil, disobedient to parents, senseless, untrustworthy, unloving, and unmerciful. Although they know God's just sentence—that those who practice such things deserve to*

> *die,—they not only do them, but* ***even applaud others who practice them*** (Romans 1:28–32 CSB emphasis added).

This describes the descending spiral of destruction we see in the modern world—a world so spiritually blind that it has lost the ability to distinguish right from wrong, resulting in the public applauding acts of evil and hatred. This spiritual delusion is the tragic, inevitable result of turning away from God.

The Believer's Stand: The Armor of God

The warnings are clear, and the consequences are being revealed daily. Instead of succumbing to the evil one, we must listen to the sound instructions from Paul in Ephesians 6:

> *Finally,* ***be strengthened by the Lord and by his vast strength.*** *Put on the* ***full armor of God*** *so that you can stand against the schemes of the devil. For our struggle is not against flesh and blood, but against the rulers, against the authorities, against the cosmic powers of this darkness, against evil, spiritual forces in the heavens. For this reason take up the full armor of God, so that you may be able to resist in the evil day, and having prepared everything, to take your stand.*
>
> ***Stand, therefore, with truth like a belt around your waist, righteousness like armor on your chest, and***

> ***your feet sandaled with readiness for the gospel of peace.*** *In every situation take up the* ***shield of faith*** *with which you can extinguish all the flaming arrows of the evil one. Take the* ***helmet of salvation*** *and the* ***sword of the Spirit****—which is the word of God. Pray at all times in the Spirit with every prayer and request, and stay alert with all perseverance and intercession for all the saints.*
>
> —Ephesians 6:10–18 CSB (emphasis added)

We all have choices to make, but thankfully, believers always have hope even though dark days are ahead. God will deliver us from evil at the appropriate time. We must continue to share the good news of salvation to a lost world that is without hope. Our answer is not in politics or government, but in the power of the gospel:

> *For* ***I am not ashamed of the gospel, because it is the power of God for salvation to everyone who believes,*** *first to the Jew, and also to the Greek. For in it the righteousness of God is revealed from faith to faith, just as it is written:* ***The righteous will live by faith****.*
>
> —Romans 1:16–17 CSB (emphasis added)

Let us live by faith, share our faith boldly, and bring those seeking the truth to a place of salvation. Just as the great Charles Spurgeon admonished the faithful in his day to get out and share the good news, "Sit not down in idleness and fold your arms in indifference to the world's woes. Behold, your compassionate Lord sends you, therefore go gladly anywhere, everywhere."[14]

[14] Charles Haddon Spurgeon, "Sheep Among Wolves," *Metropolitan Tabernacle Pulpit*, no. 23: (August 19, 1877): 12.

Thirteen:

THE BATTLE LINE IS DRAWN

Debate is dead. We now live in a very dangerous world, made even more treacherous by the fact that we are no longer allowed to disagree.

We have journeyed through the geopolitical alignments, the rise of global lawlessness, the spiritual sickness of narcissism, and the terrifying diagnosis of the reprobate mind outlined in Romans chapter 1. If the previous chapters revealed *why* the world is sick, this chapter must confront the uncomfortable truth of *what* that sickness demands of us: a choice.

The spiritual war has moved from the ethereal realm of prophecy and abstract ideology into the public square, the corporation, the classroom, and the home. The battle line is no longer theoretical; it is drawn clearly, and every person is now standing on one side or the other.

Neutrality Is Not an Option

The great lie of the modern age is that a person can be a spiritual agnostic, existing safely in the middle ground, choosing peace over confrontation. This comfort is a fantasy. Christ Himself abolished the concept of neutrality: "He that *is not with me is against me; and he that gathereth not with me scattereth abroad*" (Matthew 12:30). In a world rapidly being plunged into a state of spiritual delusion, silence is not protection; it is tacit endorsement of the descending spiral.

The choice is stark: allegiance to the Creator and His objective, eternal truth, or allegiance to the creation and the shifting sands of human-defined justice. The latter path is paved by doctrines that replace divine authority with human systems of control, judgment, and guilt.

The New Idolatry: DEI and Identity Politics

In recent years, the spirit of lawlessness has crystallized into cultural doctrines that demand total conformity. The rise of diversity, equity, and inclusion (DEI) initiatives and the enforcement of identity politics are not merely human resources programs or civil rights movements. They are the systematic construction of a new moral and social framework designed to supplant the gospel and dismantle the foundational concept of the unified human soul created in God's image.

Identity politics operates on the principle that a person's value, guilt, and moral standing are derived entirely from their membership in an assigned social group, rather than their inherent worth as an individual. This creates endless, escalating tribal warfare, pitting group against group in an irreversible power struggle—the very opposite of the unifying love of Christ.

DEI serves as the enforcement mechanism for this new spiritual paradigm, creating a hierarchy of grievance. Its primary goals are not reconciliation or true equality, which are rooted in God's impartiality, but rather the mandatory redistribution of power based on perceived historical injustices. The pursuit of "equity" (equality of outcome) over "equality" (equality of opportunity) demands a permanent system of social and economic engineering that can only function by suppressing truth and denying individual grace.

The Cost of Lawlessness: Blindness and Cancellation

The ultimate consequence of rejecting God is spiritual delusion, as referenced in the terrifying judgment described in Romans:

> *And because they did not think it worthwhile to acknowledge God,* ***God delivered them over to a***

> ***corrupt mind so that they do what is not right.*** *They are filled with all unrighteousness, evil, greed, and wickedness. They are full of envy, murder, quarrels, deceit, and malice.*
>
> —Romans 1:28–29 CSB (emphasis added)

Our world has been given over to its own deceit and immorality. This treacherous current of confusion pushes us ever farther from what is true and what is right. This over-indulgence of subterfuge, a chaos of the mind, is perpetrated upon society by a master manipulator, an enemy not to be underestimated: the father of lies.

You don't have to search to find examples; it's right in front of us, but we have to understand one thing: For those treading the broad path to destruction, they are unable to see the truth; they are blind to it, so they believe only what they are able to perceive. As believers, we see the truth through the lens provided by the indwelling Holy Spirit, which makes it difficult to understand how so many can accept the hypocritical declarations and daily contradictions espoused by our so-called experts and leaders.

Debate is dead. We are now in a very dangerous world, made even more treacherous by the fact that we are no longer allowed to disagree. Right has been declared by one side; to disagree is to commit an unforgivable act. Cross the line drawn by those who have deemed themselves above reproach and you will find yourself canceled—out of work, removed from public discourse, persona non-grata. "*Above all, be aware of this: Scoffers will come in the last days scoffing and following their own evil desires*" (2 Peter 3:3 CSB).

The prophetic words found in 2 Timothy chapter 3, where men become "*slanderers*" and "*without love for what is good*" are being fulfilled through these aggressive tactics. The goal is to silence the truth so effectively that the only voices left are those who "applaud others who practice them" as described in Romans 1:32.

The Beginning of Birth Pains

The path for the believer is clear. Jesus told us that in the last days these things would occur, but we are not to be troubled or surprised:

> *You will hear of wars and rumors of wars, but see to it that you are not alarmed.* ***Such things must happen, but the end is still to come****. Nation will rise against nation, and kingdom against kingdom. There will be famines and earthquakes in various places.* ***All these are the beginning of birth pains****.*
>
> —Matthew 24:6–8 NIV (emphasis added)

It is very important to note that Jesus referred to these times as the "*beginning of birth pains.*" Once labor has begun, the birth pains come at recurring intervals, closer together. Do you see this progression in the world right now? Various forms of conflict (murder, pestilence, pandemic, and rumors of war) are coming at an ever-increasing pace. The world is screaming for a solution, a governing power that can restore order, and the Antichrist will soon appear to offer that solution.

The Believer's Mandate: Take Up the Full Armor of God

The battle line is drawn, and the urgency of the moment is undeniable. But for the believer, the path forward is not found in politics or panic, but in the prescribed spiritual defense found in Ephesians. Remember that Paul warned us in Ephesians 6:12 that "*our struggle is not against flesh and blood, but against the rulers, against the authorities, against the cosmic powers of this darkness, against evil, spiritual forces in the heavens*" (CSB).

The battle line is drawn. Take up the full armor of God and stand. Take your stand on the side of truth, prepared to share the gospel of peace.

The Call to Faith and Patience

If you are a believer in Jesus Christ, the time to stand firm is now. If you have never taken that step of faith, surrendering to Him as Lord, now is your opportunity; please don't put it off.

Do not let yourself be distracted or discouraged; focus on Jesus and be a bright shining light in this lost world.

Remember that our fight is not against our neighbors or communities, nor is it with those who disagree with our beliefs. Our enemy would like nothing more than to invoke within us an anger at individuals or groups that call us out and mock our faith. If we give in to that desire and respond in anger, do we not become like those who call us out? They do not know the truth because they have not accepted the truth.

We must remain patient and live our lives according to Scripture. We have to share the love of Christ with those around us. If we don't, who will?

> *Dear friends, don't overlook this one fact: With the Lord one day is like a thousand years, and a thousand years like one day. The Lord does not delay his promise, as some understand delay, but is patient with you, not wanting any to perish but all to come to repentance.*
>
> —2 Peter 3:8–9 CSB

In the aftermath of the COVID-19 pandemic, the World Economic Forum (WEF) along with their partners at The Commons Project pushed their agenda to facilitate public access with confidence in health safety using a digital passport known as the CommonPass. Ultimately, the CommonPass app would allow you to access various forms of entertainment such as dining out, going to movies and sports events, and traveling by airplane. Of course, in the future, CommonPass would be integrated into the strategy to allow governments to determine what mandates, such as vaccinations, would be required of the populace for the greater good. No health passport—no freedom. As troublesome as that sounds initially, once people are conditioned to accept that level of control, it could be a small step to the harsh reality found in the book of Revelation: "*And that no man might buy or sell, save he that had the mark, or the name of the beast, or the number of his name*" (Revelation 13:17).

The book of Revelation, written by John the Apostle around AD 96, seems to hit very close to home given what we see now. I don't believe this is just a coincidence . . . do you? The proposed digital passports, such as the WEF's partnership with The Commons Project and their newly developed app, are described in an article in *MIT Technology Review*:

> Some of the terms being thrown around are confusing, like "vaccine passport." In some scenarios, your records might function like an actual passport—think of arriving at the airport in a new country, pulling out your smartphone, and scanning a digital record of your vaccination or negative test. But those records could also act like a work authorization at your job, or a pass to get into restaurants, bars, and shopping malls. Proponents argue that digital health credentials could help us get back to normal.[15]

---

[15] Lindsay Muscato and Cat Ferguson, "Will You Have to Carry a Vaccine Passport on Your Phone?" *MIT Technology Review*, December 21, 2020, https://www.technologyreview.com/2020/12/21/1015353/covid-vaccine-passport-digital-immunity-record/.

What if a book written some 2,000 years ago described this very scenario? Wouldn't that make you sit up and take notice? I think it should, just from a curiosity standpoint at the very least. However, our enemy, Satan, has been working on an alternative plan for a very long time. He knew that when these events started to unfold, he had to make sure that most of the population would think of the Bible as a book of fairytales and unreliable stories passed down through the generations. Unfortunately, his approach has worked, and many people dismiss the Bible without even taking the time to understand that it is the inspired Word of God.

Even many who "believe" in God find it hard to believe that He would have the ability to inspire the written word, which they can believe and trust. Think about that: In one sense, they believe that God is all-powerful, yet not enough to inspire people He created to write His words for us to know and obey Him. It's a world upside down to be sure, but I have complete faith in God. Like I shared above, the Bible tells us all about these events, and so far it's pretty spot on with what I see with my own eyes.

When we place our trust in Christ by simply believing that He came to this earth and gave Himself as a sacrifice for all, and was raised from the dead, we are saved. We will not suffer the coming wrath that the world will receive for rejecting our Creator. The end times are coming though no one knows when, but many things predicted in the Bible that point to the last days are lining up. I hope everyone reading this book will make the decision to stop putting their faith in human beings and bend a knee, acknowledge our Creator, and accept the redemption that is offered freely to anyone that asks by choosing to follow Jesus Christ.

For some people this sounds like crazy talk, but don't take my word for it; take some time and read what the Bible really says. I encourage you to read Romans chapter 10 and Matthew chapters 6 and 24 to find out what God is saying to you. I challenge all nonbelievers to make sure they know why they don't believe: Are you acting out of ignorance to what is said in the Bible? Is it the TV preachers or the hypocrites that dress up nice on Sunday? I don't care for many of them either, but they're not going to stand in my way of knowing the truth and experiencing God for myself. Don't use these as excuses to keep you from knowing God on a personal level. Jesus says, "*But seek ye first the kingdom of God, and his righteousness; and all these things shall be added unto you*" (Matthew 6:33). "*All these things*" includes peace, joy, love, and the promise of eternal life with our heavenly Father. Hear what Jesus says later in Matthew:

> *Enter through the narrow gate. For the gate is wide and the road broad that leads to destruction, and there are many who go through it. How narrow is the gate and difficult the road that leads to life, and few find it.*
>
> —Matthew 7:13–14 CSB

Although the gift of salvation is free to all who seek it, many will follow the broad path that leads to destruction.

Jesus tells us in these verses that the gate to eternal life with our heavenly Father is narrow and the road is difficult; few will find it. Don't be fooled into thinking that you can put this off; right now, today, this could be your final opportunity to receive salvation through Jesus Christ. Why wait any longer? Why risk your very soul? In Matthew 7:21, Jesus says, "*Not everyone who says to me, 'Lord, Lord,' will enter the kingdom of heaven*" (CSB). And in verse 23, He says, "*Then I will announce to them, 'I never knew you. Depart from me, you lawbreakers*'" (CSB).

Fourteen:

BOUGHT AT A PRICE: THE PURPOSE OF OUR EXISTENCE

If we are constantly driven by the fear of man, the fear of poverty, or the fear of failure, it means we have functionally forgotten that we have been purchased by the Creator of the universe.

Having diagnosed the sickness of the world and confronted the necessity of choosing a side, we must now address the most fundamental question of human existence: Why are we here?

This is the question that precedes all geopolitical, cultural, or prophetic concerns. It is the question every human heart, whether it acknowledges God or not, attempts to answer through career, relationships, power, or pleasure. In a world spiraling into lawlessness, understanding our God-given purpose is the one anchor that prevents us from being swept away.

The Original Intent

The answer to "Why are we here?" is not found in the complexities of the last days, but in the simplicity of the beginning. We exist by design and for a relationship. The foundational purpose of man is clear in Scripture: to glorify God and enjoy Him forever.

We were created for fellowship, which was broken by sin. Every prophecy, every war, every rising and falling kingdom, is merely the backdrop to God's grand narrative of restoring that broken relationship. "*Even every one that is called by my name: for I have created him for my glory, I have formed him; yea I have made him*" (Isaiah 43:7). Our purpose, therefore, is rooted not in what we can achieve on earth, but in whose image we reflect and whose love we accept.

Let's be clear on this: Satan is real, the spiritual battle is ongoing, the crucifixion of Christ was a bloody, humiliating and violent death . . . Jesus paid the price for our sins . . . we are bought at a price. Our hope comes through the resurrection when on the third day, God raised Jesus from the dead and He now sits at the right hand of our heavenly Father.

The Fog of the World: Forgetting the Price

If our purpose is so simple, why does it feel so impossibly difficult to maintain focus? Why do believers often live lives of chronic stress, anxiety, and spiritual weariness, sometimes indistinguishable from those who reject God entirely? The enemy does not always need a spectacular sin to destroy a believer. His most effective tactic is distraction.

We become so consumed in the everyday challenges of life that the eternal perspective is lost entirely. The persistent drumbeat of the world is deafening:

- **The bills are due** – The constant pressure of commerce and debt.
- **The job demands more** – The idol of performance and productivity.
- **The schedule is full** – The tyranny of the urgent over the important.
- **The media screams** – The endless noise of fear, anger, and grievance.

The heavy, low-hanging fog of worldly obligation and fear is designed to make us forget the profound and radical truth of our identity. It makes us forget that we are not slaves shackled to the grind but adopted children who have been ransomed from destruction. We allow the burdens of this fallen system to define our worth and consume our thoughts, thereby forgetting the ultimate price paid for our freedom.

We Were Bought at a Price

The most crucial moment in a believer's life is when they stop seeing Christ's sacrifice as merely a historical event and start seeing it as an immediate, personal valuation of their soul. God did not wait for us to be worthy; He did not wait for us to clean up our lives, secure the perfect job, or pay off our debts. He stepped into our messy reality, assessed our value, and paid the full amount: "*But God demonstrates His own love toward us, in that: While we were still sinners, Christ died for us*" (Romans 5:8 NIV).

If we are constantly driven by the fear of man, the fear of poverty, or the fear of failure, it means we have functionally forgotten that we have been purchased by the Creator of the universe. "*For ye are bought with a price: therefore glorify God in your body, and in your spirit, which are God's*" (1 Corinthians 6:20).

Because you were bought at a price, your time, your talents, and your life belong to a higher purpose—a purpose that transcends the demands of your job or the balance of your bank account. Remembering this price is the only way to break the debilitating cycle of worry and spiritual burnout.

Two Kingdoms – One Battlefield

The reason for this constant distraction and spiritual fatigue is directly connected to the enemy's purpose. If he cannot lure us with grand temptation, he will bury us under the weight of the trivial. The same demonic forces that are shaping the geopolitical alignments, fueling identity politics, and promoting global lawlessness are actively working to devour the individual soul. "*Be sober, be vigilant; because your adversary the devil, as a roaring lion, walketh about, seeking whom he may devour*" (1 Peter 5:8).

Peter's warning to be sober and vigilant is a command for clarity and focus. It means stripping away the distractions, putting aside the nonessential anxieties, and living with an acute awareness of the spiritual war being waged for your allegiance. The lion seeks to devour those who are:

- **Isolated:** Pulled away from the fellowship of the body.
- **Distracted:** So busy with earthly worries they forget to pray or read the Word.
- **Unfocused:** Living without the assurance of their eternal purpose.

We are called to stand on the side of truth, but we can only stand if we are anchored in the unwavering knowledge that our purpose is secured, our debt is paid, and our adversary is defeated by the blood of the Lamb. Do not let the fleeting anxieties of a dying world blind you to the eternal value Christ placed upon your life. Your purpose is clear: to live boldly for the One who bought you at a price.

God's Creation Story

The Bible tells us that God created day and night, He separated the land from the seas, He created all manner of creatures, both in the seas and on land. But something was missing, creation was not complete until God created man. However, we also know that God created all angelic hosts, which included the most beautiful of the angels, the one called Lucifer.

> *How art thou fallen from heaven, O Lucifer, son of the morning! how art thou cut down to the ground, which didst weaken the nations!*
>
> —Isaiah 14:12

> *Son of man, lament for the king of Tyre and say to him, "This is what the Lord God says: You were the seal of perfection, full of wisdom and perfect in beauty. You were in Eden, the garden of God. Every kind of precious stone covered you: carnelian, topaz, and diamond, beryl, onyx, and jasper, lapis lazuli, turquoise and emerald. Your mountings and settings were crafted in gold; they were prepared on the day you were created. You were an anointed guardian cherub, for I had appointed you. You were on the holy mountain of God; you walked among the fiery stones. From the day you were created you were blameless in your ways until wickedness was found in you. Through the abundance of your trade*, **you were filled with violence, and you sinned. So**

> **I expelled you in disgrace from the mountain of God, and banished you, guardian cherub, from among the fiery stones.**"
>
> —Ezekiel 28:12–16 CSB (emphasis added)

From this, we know that God's perfect creation, including man, was set on a collision course of good against evil, as Lucifer was cast out of heaven, along with the legion of angels that followed. Satan, as he became known, so despised God that he made it his mission to seek and devour all mankind like a hungry lion.

Why Did Lucifer and Humans Fall?

Why did Satan fall? It can be summed up in one word, pride. "*Your heart became proud because of your beauty; for the sake of your splendor you corrupted your wisdom. So I threw you down to the ground*" (Ezekiel 28:17 CSB).

It was through the sin of pride that Satan fell from grace and turned on mankind as we read when he encountered Eve in the garden. In Genesis chapter 3, Satan used the serpent to tempt Eve by contradicting God. The instructions about the tree of the knowledge of good and evil were clear: God forbid them to eat. Satan tickled Eve's ears by deceiving her into thinking that if she ate of this tree, she would become as God with all knowledge and wisdom. Adam and Eve both ate the fruit of the tree and became aware that they were naked, and they hid from the Lord. When God came into the garden in the evening He called out to Adam, "Where are you?" God knew where Adam was but in calling out to him, He was indicating that they had become separated by sin.

God asked Adam what he had done, and he blamed Eve and, in a sense, he blamed God as he explained the fruit was given to him by the woman that God had created. At this point, the perfect creation of God was corrupted; sin had entered man, and this sinful nature would be passed through every generation. Adam did not immediately repent of his sin for disobeying God's command regarding the tree of knowledge; instead, he made excuses and blamed Eve; in so doing, all mankind suffers the consequences of that day.

What Is God's Purpose for Us?

Why did God create us if we were doomed to failure and sin? Was God lonely? Was He taken by surprise that Man sinned against Him? Satan would love for us to believe that he was able to sneak into the garden of Eden and ruin creation without God having any knowledge of what was happening. But that is not the case. Although man was created by God and given a free will, it is a mistake to think that man has autonomy over God's plans or that sin was introduced by happenstance forcing God to come up with a new plan to rectify the situation. God knows future events as demonstrated throughout the Bible, both in prophesy and by the very words of Christ who foretold His own destiny.

Furthermore, we know that God not only possesses foreknowledge of events, but He also plans those events and puts them into action.

> *Remember the former things of old: for I am God, and there is none else; I am God, and there is none like me, declaring the end from the beginning and from ancient times the things that are not yet done, saying, My counsel shall stand, and I will do all my pleasure.*
>
> —Isaiah 46:9–11

We see His omniscience throughout Scripture as the prophets were given knowledge of things to come according to God's plans and purposes. His omniscience is also revealed through Jesus as He foretold the disciples of His coming crucifixion and resurrection among other things. Jesus told the disciples at the Last Supper of Judas's betrayal and Peter's coming denial. Therefore, we know without any doubt that nothing surprises God. Not only does He know the future, but He also plans for it and carries out His purposes according to His will. So, why did God create mankind? I think this question is best answered by C. S. Lewis:

God did not make us because He was bored, lonely, or had run out of things to do. He created us to be the objects of His love! Sometimes our actions make us unlovely, but we are never unloved. And because God loves us–we have value. And nobody can take that value away. God's love revealed at Calvary fastens itself onto flawed creatures like us, and for reasons none of us can ever quite figure out, makes us precious and valued beyond calculation. This is love beyond reason. And this is the love with which God loves us.[16]

When we try to fathom this abundant love, we encounter frustration as we struggle to comprehend God's true purposes for our lives:

> *No, in all these things we are more than conquerors through him who loved us. For I am sure that neither death nor life, nor angels nor rulers, nor things present nor things to come, nor powers, nor height nor depth, nor any other created thing will be able to separate us from the love of God that is in Christ Jesus our Lord.*
>
> —Romans 8:37–39 CSB

God's Salvation Plan

This brings us to the amazing grace extended to all mankind from our Creator. Satan introduced sin and all evil into this world, and he continues his all-out assault without ceasing. If Satan hates God, then why does he attack us? "*So God created man in his own image, in the image of God he created him; male and female created he them*" (Genesis 1:27).

Because of God's unending love for us, we have value in His sight, and this value causes Satan to seethe with rage

---

[16] C. S. Lewis, *The Four Loves* (Harvest/Harcourt Brace Jovanovich, 1960), 127.

against us. We are created in the very image of God. We are caught in a spiritual battle, a tug of war for our very souls. Yet in all this, God also created the perfect plan of salvation. We are not hopelessly lost, for we have a way out, not because of anything we do. The very love that brought about our creation is why Jesus died as a living sacrifice in our place to cover all our transgressions. God values each of us so much that he provided a way for our redemption so that we can spend eternity with Him. "*For God so loved the world, that He gave his only begotten Son, that whosoever believeth in Him shall not perish, but have everlasting life*" (John 3:16). The Apostle Paul has this to say about how much God values us: "*Do you not know that your bodies are temples of the Holy Spirit, who is in you, whom you have received from God? You are not your own; you were bought at a price. Therefore honor God with your bodies*" (1 Corinthians 6:19–20 NIV).

We give ourselves over to God completely when we accept salvation through the death and resurrection of Jesus. We are no longer our own, we belong to God. Jesus took our rightful consequences upon himself, and though he was without sin, he paid the debt that we could not pay. Jesus laid bare his back and took the scourging of a Roman soldier's whip. He carried our cross through the streets along the *via dolorosa*, or the way of suffering and was nailed to that cross at Golgotha where he died a slow, agonizing death for our sins. That is the price of our salvation; Jesus paid the cost so that we can find redemption instead of paying the wages of iniquities, which is death and eternal separation from our Creator.

Unfortunately today, a new religion has sprung up and is enjoying great success as the purveyors of this "gospel" share a message of love of self and the good life with little, if any, mention of God or the consequences of sin and the payment that Christ made on our behalf. This watered-down form of religion allows people to hold onto a form of godliness without dealing with the baggage of sin. After all, they say, "Who are we to judge others?"

Paul spoke of this coming age and warned against it in 2 Timothy 3:2–5, saying that "*people will be lovers of self, lovers of money, boastful and proud, . . . holding to a form of godliness but denying its power. Avoid such people*" (CSB). Our mission as believers in Christ is to share the true gospel message with compassion for those that have not found salvation in the hope that they will repent and experience the gift of redemption. "*For all have sinned, and come short of the glory of God*" (Romans 3:23).

The good news continues in Romans 3:24–26:

> *Being justified freely by his grace through the redemption that is in Christ Jesus: whom God hath set forth to be a propitiation through faith in his blood, to declare his righteousness for the remission of sins that are past, through the forbearance of God; to declare, I say, at this time his righteousness: that he might be just and the justifier of him which believeth in Jesus.*

We are instructed by Christ to share our faith, so that the world may come to know the true grace of God and draw others into the Kingdom of God. As C. S. Lewis wrote, "If you aim for heaven, you will get earth thrown in: Aim at earth and you will get neither."[17]

Where is the Kingdom of God? In Jesus's day, the people had no desire to put their faith in Christ, have their hearts changed, turn away from their sins, and love others. They wanted earthly justice and revenge. In many ways we see this same misguided emphasis in our churches today. People want governments to conform to our sense of justice; in America, we stand on the steps of the Supreme Court and shout for right and push away those who need to hear the message of salvation the most. We say we want revival, but our actions often show that we want political change and justice even more.

As believers Matthew chapter 28 calls us to the great commission of sharing the love of Christ with everyone, so that they might be drawn to repentance. Paul extolled the virtues of patience and gentleness in the following passage:

> *The Lord's servant must not quarrel, but must be gentle to everyone, able to teach, and patient, instructing his opponents with gentleness. Perhaps God will grant them repentance leading them to the knowledge of the truth.*
>
> —2 Timothy 2:24–25 CSB

[17] Lewis, *Mere Christianity* (HarperCollins, 2001), 27.

Laying Hold of the Kingdom of God

In this chapter, we have traveled a long way, from creation through redemption, asking questions about purpose in life and living in God's amazing grace. So let's take hold of this great redemptive story and share the passion of our Savior and Lord. Our purpose is to strive to be like Jesus, to accept God's unconditional love and to share that love with one another. Paul eloquently taught that we should turn away from impurity and ignorance:

> *But that is not how you came to know Christ, assuming you heard about him and were taught by him, as the truth is in Jesus, to take off your former way of life, the old self that is corrupted by deceitful desires, to be renewed in the spirit of your minds, and to put on the new self, the one created according to God's likeness in righteousness and purity of the truth.*
>
> —Ephesians 4:20–24 CSB

> *No foul language should come from your mouth, but only what is good for building up someone in need, so that it gives grace to those who hear. And don't grieve God's Holy Spirit. You were sealed by him for the day of redemption. Let all bitterness, anger and wrath, shouting and slander be removed from you, along with all malice. And be kind and compassionate to one another, forgiving one another, just as God also forgave you in Christ.*
>
> —Ephesians 4:29–32 CSB

We have found the kingdom of God; it resides within the hearts of believers by the grace of our heavenly Father. So, let's seek revival, starting in our own hearts and asking God to search our hearts and minds and show us His will as we journey through this life in preparation for the next. We know that God's principles and moral foundations work, but let's not become distracted in our pursuit of change, expecting a lost world to adapt to our ways. To bring about change and turn the world toward God, we should focus on reaching people's hearts, not on influencing the institutions of man's creation. We can all be one through Jesus Christ; we are all created in God's image, and we all have great value in His sight.

Question for Believers

You have seen the signs, understood the spiritual diagnosis, and been equipped with the call to action. You have been created in God's image and have been reminded of your divine purpose and immense worth in Christ. How will you choose to live the precious, purchased life you have been given as you move toward the finish line?

Question for the Nonbeliever

You have been shown the signs, the spiritual diagnosis, and been told that you are created in God's image. According to Scripture, you have immense worth in Christ; yet, you have not chosen to accept the One who gave His life for you. What would you consider the main impediments holding you back from taking that step of faith toward Jesus? While you consider that question, I encourage you to continue this journey with me—as a friend and neighbor—in the sincere hope that you will find that narrow path that leads to peace and forgiveness.

Fifteen:

THE HIGHEST COMMAND: LOVE AND THE CLARITY OF TRUTH

This is the central deception of the enemy: convincing the world that truth and love are opposites when, in the Kingdom of God, they are two sides of the same coin.

We have discussed our purpose and the spiritual war raging for our allegiance. Now, we must turn to the highest calling placed upon every believer—a calling that serves as both our greatest defensive and offensive weapon in these last days: Love.

When a legal expert attempted to trap Jesus, he asked Him to identify the most important command in the Law.

Jesus did not provide a complex theological answer; instead, He gave us the definitive blueprint for purpose and action:

> *"The most important one," answered Jesus, "is this: 'Hear, O Israel: The Lord our God, the Lord is one. Love the Lord your God with all your heart and with all your soul and with all your mind and with all your strength.' The second is this: '**Love your neighbor as yourself**.' There is no commandment greater than these."*
>
> —Mark 12:29–31 NIV (emphasis added)

These two commands are inseparable. You cannot claim to love the Creator if you fail to love His creation, and you cannot truly love your neighbor without first knowing and being obedient to the God who defines what love truly is. This chapter explores the higher calling to love your neighbor as yourself and clarifies how that love must be expressed in a world that intentionally misunderstands the word.

The World's Misguided Mantra of "Love"

Today, the word *love* has been hollowed out and redefined by the world into a concept that serves self-justification rather than sacrifice. Many nonbelievers question the Bible and try to justify their sinful ways by hiding behind a misguided mantra of tolerance, claiming, "God is love; therefore anything done in the name of love, or done out of self-acceptance, must be fine." This worldly version of "love" is characterized by:

- **Exclusion of Truth:** It avoids any statement that implies moral correction or disagreement with personal choices.
- **Affirmation of Self:** It prioritizes the comfort and immediate desires of the individual over their eternal well-being.
- **Rejection of Sacrifice:** It demands acceptance without requiring repentance, accountability, or the difficult work of discipleship.

In this context, believers who dare to speak the uncompromising truth of Scripture—that sin leads to death, and salvation is found only through Christ—are immediately branded as "unloving, intolerant, and hateful." This is the central deception of the enemy: convincing the world that truth and love are opposites when, in the Kingdom of God, they are two sides of the same coin.

The Defining Difference: Truthful Love

True, biblical love, *Agape* love, does not tolerate that which ultimately destroys the soul. If you see a neighbor walking blindly toward the edge of a cliff, the loving response is not to quietly tolerate their path, but to shout a warning. If you see a neighbor drinking poison, the loving act is not to affirm their choice, but to offer the antidote.

The poison we see pervading our society—the violence, deceit, malice, and cancellation—is all a symptom of sin, which ultimately leads to spiritual death. Therefore, the greatest, most profound act of love a believer can offer is the antidote: the gospel of Jesus Christ.

When believers share the truth of God—the reality of sin, the necessity of repentance, and the free gift of redemption—we are sharing our love for them, hoping they will turn from evil and find the joy and peace that only comes through a relationship with Jesus.

> *For the word of God is living and active. Sharper than any double-edged sword, it penetrates even to dividing soul and spirit, joints and marrow; it judges the thoughts and attitudes of the heart.*
>
> —Hebrews 4:12 NIV

The truth *must* pierce the heart for healing to begin. We are not called to be critics of the world, but physicians who offer the cure. Our words should be firm in conviction but soaked in compassion, knowing that we, too, were once spiritually blind and lost.

Love Requires Boldness, Not Silence

The fear of being labeled "unloving" is one of the most effective tools the enemy uses to silence the Church. It is this fear that causes many believers to retreat into spiritual isolation, keeping the most precious, life-saving truth hidden within their own hearts. This reluctance is not an act of love; it is an act of spiritual cowardice.

The Apostle Paul, who endured relentless persecution, never wavered in his belief that sharing the gospel was the ultimate expression of care for humanity: "*For I am not ashamed of the gospel, because it is the power of God that brings salvation to everyone who believes*" (Romans 1:16 NIV). Our love for our neighbor must override our fear of cancellation. We must remember that while a worldly rejection might cost us a job, silence might cost our neighbor their soul.

It sounds easy enough when you call for everyone to love one another, but if you don't truly understand the concept of love from a biblical standpoint, you miss the point entirely. This lack of understanding is common when a lost people who have rejected God pick up the Bible to command that we love one another as we love ourselves. Their version of love is often merged with the worldly concepts of tolerance and acceptance. This is where it all goes off the rails and leads to confusion and a misappropriation of ideals shoved down our proverbial throats.

The love of God is uniquely described by C. S. Lewis as a charitable love that reaches the highest distinctions of sacrifice and mercy. Our heavenly Father is love, and it is very important to understand why we are given this paternal reference in our spiritual relationship to the Creator. Being mankind's perfect Father, God does not lay out boundaries, laws, and guidelines to punish us; on the contrary, as with any good parent, He knows the traps that await us and directs us away from things that will ultimately destroy our souls should we choose certain paths in life. His is an all-encompassing love, a sacrificial selfless love. Because He knows that we are born into a sinful and fallen world, this love provides redemption through Christ's ultimate sacrifice, and He gives us His written Word to guide us through life with built-in protections to help us avoid the destructive and damaging consequences of our own sinful nature.

The world's recipe of tolerance and acceptance mixed with pseudo "biblical love," often accompanied by the misused passages of Scriptures such as 1 Corinthians chapter 13, leads many inside and outside the church, down a dark path of compromise. What might seem right on the surface almost always leads to destruction.

> *Love is patient, love is kind. It does not envy, it does not boast, it is not proud. It does not dishonor others, it is not self-seeking, it is not easily angered, it keeps no record of wrongs. Love does not delight in evil but rejoices with the truth. It always protects, always trusts, always hopes, always perseveres.*
>
> —1 Corinthians 13:4–7 NIV

Without a true knowledge and understanding of God's love, those who cherry-pick verses in an exercise of self-serving justification, risk their very being in the process. How many times has a nonbeliever tried to guilt or shame Christians by referencing these verses, misrepresenting the portion that love "*keeps no record of wrongs*" while ignoring the follow-up that "*love does not delight in evil but rejoices with the truth.*" Love becomes weaponized as a justification to allow for the pursuit of all pleasures without boundaries and emboldens those that hate God to try to shut down the influence of good over evil.

This mixed message, the co-opting of Scripture for self-serving purposes, has found its way inside the Church, and those who should be leaders in the faith are buying into this desire to be inclusive and all loving, which is nothing more than choosing popularity over purpose.

What Is Love?

In his radio broadcasts on the BBC in the late 1950s, later transcribed into a book titled *The Four Loves*, C. S. Lewis shared his philosophical and theological differentiation of what he categorized as the four types of love: affection, friendship, eros, and charity. He identified affection, friendship, and eros as "natural" loves and gave charity a higher distinction of love that is defined by the maxim, "*God is love.*" This is the premise that underlies all his arguments about what true love is. While outlining the benefits and potential dangers found within each type, Lewis demonstrated how they illuminate distinct aspects of God's character.

In the Gospel of Luke, Jesus defines what love is in no uncertain terms and once again, we are reminded that His standard is set very high. He made His point by sharing the parable of the good Samaritan; before you read the parable, it helps to understand the backdrop of this narrative. In Jesus's day, Samaritans were despised in all neighboring regions of Judea; they were seen as heretics because they worshiped idols and because of their mixed ethnicity and perceived ignorance. In today's terminology they would be considered "deplorables."

> *And Jesus answering said: A certain man went down from Jerusalem to Jericho, and fell among thieves, which stripped him of his raiment, and wounded him, and departed, leaving him half dead. And by chance there came down a certain priest that road way: and when he saw him, he passed by on the other side. And likewise a Levite, when he was at the place, came and looked on him, and passed by on the other side. But a certain Samaritan, as he journeyed, came where he was: and when he saw him, he had compassion on him, and went to him, and bound up his wounds, pouring in oil and wine, and set him on his own beast, and brought him to an inn, and took care of him. And on morrow when he departed, he took out two pence, and gave them to the host, and said unto him, Take care of him; and whatsoever thou spendest more, when I come again, I will repay thee. Which now of these three, thinkest thou was neighbour to him that fell among the thieves?" And he said,* He that shewed

> mercy on him. Then said Jesus unto him, Go and do thou likewise.
>
> —Luke 10:30–37

Examine these words closely; this self-righteous jurist posed the question thinking to justify himself, but Jesus gives the example through a parable and then with great precision turns the question around, "*so which of these three do you think was neighbour to him*?" In other words, Jesus is asking who proved he was a good neighbor by his actions. The obvious answer is that the man who showed mercy and kindness to the stranger in need was a good neighbor. Jesus, in turn, calls all believers to "*Go and do thou likewise.*" Each of us is someone's neighbor, and we are to see biblical love as an extension of grace, a life of humble compassion and putting others needs ahead of our own. That is what it means to love others, our neighbors, as ourselves.

The most complete act of love is demonstrated in Jesus Christ who laid down His life for His friends. Even in His final hours as Christ prepares for the Last Supper, He demonstrates humble servitude by getting on His knees and washing His disciples' feet. Jesus, the true Son of God, shows his mercy and love for all mankind on bended knee.

The Highest Command and the Final Days

As the birth pains intensify (chapter 13) and the world accelerates its descent into lawlessness (chapter 5), the darkness will only make the light of Christ shine brighter. Our mandate is simple:

- **Maintain Focus:** Keep your eyes fixed on the price that was paid for you. This prevents the world's worries from consuming you.
- **Wear the Armor:** Stand firm in the truth, righteousness, and the gospel of peace. This provides the posture for sharing.
- **Speak in Love:** Deliver the ultimate act of love—the clarity of God's Word—to those who are lost.

Loving your neighbor as yourself means loving their soul more than their feelings. It means refusing to lie to them about the stakes of this life. It means offering the peace that surpasses all understanding to those consumed by the world's chaos. This is our final, urgent mission.

Question for the Believer

Knowing that true love requires truth and that the world will call you hateful for sharing it, are you prepared to love your neighbor enough to risk the world's disapproval?

Sixteen:

THE GREAT SEDUCTION: COMFORT AND THE SILENT CHURCH

But what if the greatest threat to our witness isn't persecution from the outside, but lukewarmness on the inside?

We have established the price paid for our souls and the true, uncompromising nature of the love we owe our neighbor. The following question, then, is intensely personal: Are we living like people who have been bought at a price, or people who simply bought a ticket to a weekly show?

For generations of believers living in the Western world, especially in the era following the devastation of the world wars, a kind of cultural truce was brokered. Churches flourished in the safety and stability of democratic, capitalist societies. We began to enjoy a life of comfort, prosperity, and predictability that our ancestors, who often faced persecution or genuine physical want, could scarcely imagine. But in this ease, a great and subtle seduction has taken hold of the Church: complacency.

When Comfort Becomes the Idol

We love things to be a certain way, don't we? We seek the comfortable, the predictable, and the sociable within the walls of our churches. We expect our places of worship to be acoustically perfect, visually appealing, and emotionally reassuring. We prefer a Christianity that is a pleasant addition to a happy life, rather than a radical commitment to a life of sacrifice. This preference for comfort has bled into our spiritual posture:

- We seek the *social* hour, not the *spiritual* labor.
- We prefer the *predictable* sermon, not the *piercing* truth.
- We prioritize *personal happiness* over *prophetic urgency*.

The modern church risks becoming a place of convenient assembly rather than a mobilization center for a war-torn world. We attend church for an hour or two each week, put away our Bibles with a satisfied sigh, and then go about our business, pursuing nothing more than our own individualized, personal happiness. We assume that because we feel good, God is pleased. But what if the greatest threat to our witness isn't persecution from the outside, but lukewarmness on the inside?

Can I Get a Witness?

In a time when the world is in desperate need of a spiritual anchor, many of us, the very people called to be the light of the world, are keeping our lamps hidden under a bushel of personal ambition and domestic comfort. The contrast between our prosperous Christian lives and the spiritual poverty of the world has never been starker.

The evidence of the deepening darkness is everywhere. As we explored in previous chapters, the evil spirit of the antichrist is already at work in the world. Nonbelievers are floundering in darkness, lashing out in anger, bitterness, and utter hopelessness because they have no foundation upon which to stand. They are seeking desperately for peace in all the wrong places. The silence of a comfortable church is deafening to a dying world.

I Ask Again, Can I Get a Witness?

If we, the redeemed, the ransomed, the ones who claim to have the very Spirit of God dwelling within us are not actively shining the light of Jesus Christ through our witness and testimony, then who will do it for us? The answer is simple and terrifying: No one.

No television preacher, no large ministry budget, and no Sunday morning performance can replace the raw, authentic witness of a believer who has taken up their cross and lives a life set apart in the presence of the lost.

The Higher Calling: A Challenge to Every Believer

This is not a message for the pastorate alone; it is a challenge to all who call themselves by Christ's name. We must honestly look at ourselves: Are we following the calling from our Savior?

Jesus called us to be disciples, which means disciplined ones. Discipleship is not a one-time decision; it is a daily, relentless application of intentional spiritual habits. The life of a genuine follower of Christ requires us to step out of the comfort of the spectator section and onto the field of battle.

We must make the deliberate choice to get into the Word daily, not just for knowledge, but for transformation. We must couple our study with serious prayer, which requires time and vulnerability, allowing God to expose the complacency in our own hearts. Finally, we must walk with the Lord in service, actively seeking opportunities to take up our cross to follow Christ.

To take up your cross is to deny yourself (Matthew 16:24) and the comfortable, predictable life you have curated and embrace the mission of rescue for those drowning in the darkness. Our witness is the one thing that gives hope to a hopeless generation. Do not let the luxury of your life today steal the urgency of your mission tomorrow.

Question for the Believer

What earthly comfort are you currently prioritizing that is hindering your calling to discipleship and silencing your necessary witness to the world?

Seventeen:

THE COST OF CONVICTION: STEPHEN AND THE PROMISE OF ENDURANCE

The world is looking for answers, but they are searching in the wrong places. World governments will not provide the solutions they seek.

We are living in a world defined by volatility and crisis. Wild extremes in weather, record-breaking temperatures, floods, disease, and societal unrest—the list goes on, a relentless barrage of instability that the world calls "unprecedented." Yet, this list is not unfamiliar to anyone who reads the Bible. These are the birth pangs described by Jesus, the very signs indicating that the season is rapidly changing.

The magnitude of the darkness can be overwhelming. Even for believers, it is getting harder to remain hopeful, harder to be the salt and light so desperately needed in this lost world. The pressure to conform, to be silent, or to compromise is immense. This pressure is not a surprise; it is a promise.

The Blueprint for Endurance

We are all familiar with the warnings given by the Apostle Paul in 2 Timothy chapter 3, which starts with the grim introduction: "*There will be terrible times in the last days*" (NIV). We are living those terrible times at this very moment. But we must fix our attention on a later portion of that chapter, for it serves as a powerful reminder that our hope is not lost, that God is in control, and that these things must take place for His perfect will to play out. Paul wrote these eloquent words to his young protégé:

> *You, however, know all about my teaching, my way of life, my purpose, faith, patience, love, endurance, persecutions, sufferings—what kinds of things happened to me in Antioch, Iconium and Lystra, the persecutions I endured. Yet the Lord rescued me from all of them.* ***In fact, everyone who wants to live a godly life in Christ Jesus will be persecuted,*** *while evildoers and impostors will go from bad to worse, deceiving and being deceived. But as for you, continue in what you*

> *have learned and have become convinced of, because you know those from whom you learned it, and how from infancy you have known the Holy Scriptures, which are able to make you wise for salvation through faith in Christ Jesus. All Scripture is God-breathed and is useful for teaching, rebuking, correcting and training in righteousness, so that the servant of God may be thoroughly equipped for every good work.*
>
> —2 Timothy 3:10–17 NIV (emphasis added)

This is an assurance, not a warning: "*Everyone who wants to live a godly life in Christ Jesus will be persecuted.*" This statement eliminates the possibility of a comfortable, quiet, or universally approved Christianity (chapter 16). Paul knew this firsthand; he was the man who preached the gospel at Lystra, healed the crippled, and was then stoned by an angry mob who dragged his body outside the city gates, assuming him dead. Yet, Paul rose up from that extreme persecution and continued to preach, focused solely on Christ, eventually becoming a martyr himself.

But Paul was not the first martyr. When Stephen, the first to pay the ultimate price for his witness, was killed, Paul—then known as Saul of Tarsus, a zealot and strong enforcer for the Pharisees—was present and accounted for at this terrible event.

Stephen: The First Martyr and The Highest Perspective

Stephen, a man described as being full of the Holy Spirit and wisdom, was taken before the court of the Sanhedrin and falsely accused of blasphemy. The High Priest asked Stephen, "*Are these charges true?*"

Given this opportunity, Stephen did not try to save himself. His faith was unshakable, and his commitment was absolute. He used the platform to preach the entire history of Israel, culminating in a powerful, undeniable accusation of the religious leaders' sin:

> *Was there ever a prophet your ancestors did not persecute? They even killed those who predicted the coming of the Righteous One.* ***And now you have betrayed and murdered him****—you who have received the law that was given through angels but have not obeyed it.*
>
> —Acts 7:52–53 NIV (emphasis added)

When the religious leaders heard this, they were enraged and gnashed their teeth at him. But Stephen, in that moment of ultimate earthly danger, experienced the greatest peace known to mankind:

> *But Stephen, full of the Holy Spirit, looked up to heaven and saw the glory of God, and Jesus standing at the right hand of God. "Look," he said, "I see heaven open and the Son of Man standing at the right hand of God."*
>
> —Acts 7:55–56 NIV

While Jesus is typically described as seated in authority, Stephen saw Him standing—perhaps rising to receive His faithful servant. This heavenly vision provided the strength for Stephen's final, most profound act: As he was being stoned, he fell on his knees and cried out, "*Lord, do not hold this sin against them*" (Acts 7:59 NIV). Imagine being able to sincerely call out to God with such forgiveness while you are being murdered. This is the difference between a worldly perspective focused on self and an eternal perspective fixed on Christ. Stephen fulfilled the ultimate command of loving his neighbor even as they enacted violence upon him.

Our Work Until He Gathers Us

Believer, if you feel the weight of the world upon your shoulders and are burdened to the point of simply wanting to give up, remember Stephen. Don't give up. Stand up!

Yes, it is hard to walk in faith in today's dark world, but we are not of this world; our Savior's kingdom is our home, and we will be gathered there soon enough. But until that time, we have work to do.

We have an obligation to honor all those who have gone before us by remaining focused on the One who delivered us from all sin: Jesus Christ. The world is looking for answers, but they are searching in the wrong places. World governments will not provide the solutions they need. Those who ignore the truth will soon welcome a ruler who brings temporary solutions—the one prophesied to usher in a time so horrible, the "*abomination of desolation*" (Daniel 9:27 CSB). Jesus described this time as one of great tribulation, such as has not been since the beginning of the world, nor will there ever be again.

- **Believers:** Look up and know that God is with you; then step up and be the light in this dark world. We gain our strength through the daily, disciplined rhythm of prayer and study of the Word.
- **Nonbelievers:** Time is running out. The world has no answers, and unless you come to repentance, you will face a time of great tribulation like no other. The time to believe is now.

Question for the Believer

If your witness put your comfort and safety at risk today, would your reaction be anger toward your persecutors or the forgiveness and hope of Stephen?

Eighteen:

WHY JESUS? CONFRONTING THE SPIRIT OF SKEPTICISM

Through our salvation in Jesus Christ, we have gained that peace that surpasses all human understanding. Let this light of Christ shine brightly so that a lost world may see it, desire it, and come to believe in Him.

After confronting the comfort that threatens to spoil the modern Church and recognizing the cost of true conviction, we must now address the enemy's most sophisticated weapon: intellectual arrogance. The question is simple, yet profound: Why Jesus?

In a world that celebrates scientific advancement and champions secular materialism, faith is often not just dismissed; it's actively mocked. Consider these comments by noted atheist, zoologist, and author Richard Dawkins stating his take on religion: "Religious faith is above all a sign of faulty thinking, of ignorance." Dawkins stated mission is to "educate the ill-informed out of their mistakes," breaking down religion as nothing more than "an organized license to be acceptably stupid."[18] His combativeness is not merely a philosophical stance; it's a mission: to promote science and demolish religion.

The Myth of Scientific Infallibility

Dawkins's dismissal of theology as "acceptably stupid" forces us to ask: Is Christianity truly a faith of the uninformed, or is this overly simplistic dismissal the real act of ignorance? If we accept the "uninformed" label, then it must also be applied to some of the greatest minds in scientific history who held a profound belief in God, including Galileo, Copernicus, and Isaac Newton. It would also have to include Albert Einstein, who famously stated, "Science without religion is lame, religion without science is blind."[19]

Atheists often seek to debate believers armed with the

[18] Ed Ceasar, "Is Richard Dawkins Destroying His Reputation?" *The Guardian*, June 2015, www.theguardian.com/science/2015/jun/09/is-richard-dawkins-destroying-his-reputation.

[19] Albert Einstein, *Out of My Later Years* (Philosophical Library, 1950), 41.

"facts" of science while deriding the Bible as nothing more than stories. But to claim science as "fact" versus theology as "fiction" is to dismiss the very foundation of scientific theory itself—the gathering of factual data to support a specific *proposition*.

Consider the infamous case of the noted mathematician Urbain Jean Joseph Le Verrier.[20] In the mid-nineteenth century, the orbit of Mercury around the Sun did not fit any known scientific theory. Based on his brilliant mathematical formulations, Le Verrier determined that another planet must exist between the Sun and Mercury, influencing its orbit through gravitational energy. He named this yet undiscovered planet Vulcan. Le Verrier's theory became widely accepted, putting the scientific contradiction to rest. It became scientific "fact" of the day, leading hundreds of European astronomers to report "sightings" of this new celestial body. When Le Verrier died in 1877, he was hailed as the man who discovered Vulcan.

However, the existence of Vulcan, supported by Le Verrier's scientific "facts" and the hundreds of "confirmed" sightings, evaporated in 1915 upon the publication of Einstein's theory of relativity. Einstein's new data explained Mercury's orbital oddities through the curvature of spacetime, rendering

---

[20] Ross Pomeroy, "The Real History of the Planet Vulcan: How a Planet's Death Birthed Relativity," *Real Clear Science*, April 7, 2015, https://www.realclearscience.com/blog/2015/04/the_real_history_of_the_fake_planet_vulcan.html.

the need for Vulcan nonexistent. The scientific community quietly declared, "Nothing to see here, move along."

The educated elite will justify the retirement of Vulcan as an example of progress—the ability of science to admit mistakes and evolve. They credit their ability to keep an open mind, contrasting it with the perceived "static Word of God," which they equate with closed-mindedness. It seems extremely hypocritical to embrace science as "fact" even as they continually change their own outcomes, while theology, which has no need to change the Word of God, is equated to a closed-minded worldview simply for its unfailing integrity.

Science is not without great merit; we do not choose religion over science. We embrace the advancements in science that allow us to improve our lives and, in many cases, come to a greater understanding of how magnificent the work of God is in the world He created. But while science continues to evolve, standing alone, unchanged through the millennia, is the undeniable Word of God.

Therefore, I ask you, believer or not: Based on common sense, where would you rather cast your fortunes—on an ever-changing theory of scientific proposition or the unchanging Word of God?

The Truth Behind the Anger

Why would a nonbeliever seek to know more about Christ? Why not simply accept the status quo and be content with the material world? The answer is this: Whether we are brought up in church or not, we all at some point seek to know more about the spiritual world because we are living spirits, eternal beings, made in the image of our Creator.

Atheists often lash out against children being exposed to religion, fearing that it forces beliefs upon them at an impressionable age. Richard Dawkins, in his outrage during one of his many public debates, asks: "How dare you force your dopey unsubstantiated superstitions on children too young to resist. How dare you."[21] Yet, these very same proponents of atheism are eager to push the theory of evolution as definitive fact to these same young children. This isn't about offense over "pushing" belief; it's about a spiritual struggle to gain influence over children at an early age. Dawkins wants to crush religion, and that clarity is telling.

The bitterness and severe anger that the concept of God provokes in so many atheists reveal the truth: A great spiritual battle is playing out all around us. We are not just a random collection of atoms; we share in this spiritual existence as beings created by God and given free will. The anger stems not from the offense of religion in the public square (which is virtually nonexistent in modern America), but from the fact that God is still there in all His glory.

Atheists postulate that belief in God shuts off all reasonable thought and take the easy way out. Yet, in their own

---

[21] Daniel Rowe, "Telling Children They Belong to a Religion Is Child Abuse," EP4: Richard Dawkins/Rabbi Daniel Rowe, Aish UK online, April 8, 2021.

arrogance and refusal to acknowledge their Creator, they are not seekers of knowledge; they are running from the truth.

This avoidance of truth manifests itself in the devaluation of life. When recently asked how to handle a pregnancy if the unborn child had Down Syndrome, Richard Dawkins offered a chilling and flippant reply: "Abort it and try again. It would be immoral to bring it into the world if you have the choice."[22] This cold retort—to toss one life aside and "give it another try"— demonstrates the natural progression of a worldview that has moved as far as possible from the complete and unconditional love of our Creator.

Our Witness: Peace, not Protest

What is the role of the Church in getting the message of faith and forgiveness to this lost world? We are well-versed in the Great Commission found in Matthew chapter 28, which calls us to make disciples of all nations. The question remains: How do we apply this charge today? Some respond to persecution with litigation and political action. Others engage in charity. Many others simply occupy a church pew once a week and go home.

We must remember the charge from the Apostle Peter: "*But in your hearts revere Christ as Lord.* ***Always be prepared to give an answer to everyone who asks you to give the***

[22] Kathleen Hawkins, "Richard Dawkins: 'Immoral' not to Abort Down's foetuses," BBC News, August 21, 2014.

reason for the hope that you have. But do this with gentleness and respect" (1 Peter 3:15 NIV emphasis added). Notice the sequence: we are asked to give the reason for the hope they see in us. This means our daily activities—at work, running errands, or conducting business—must be a silent, yet powerful living testimony to our faith. "*Let your light so shine before men, that they may see your good works, and glorify your Father which is in heaven*" (Matthew 5:16).

If a nonbeliever only hears from Christians when we are angry, litigating, or shouting protests, why would they ever want to be a part of that belief? An angry street preacher with a bullhorn, condemning sinners, may have the best intentions, but his message is lost in his own anger and disgust aimed at sinners. That presentation will never win a soul to Christ. Our good deeds should come because of our salvation, not to earn God's favor. Paul reminds us it is by our faith in Christ, through the grace of God, that we are saved, not by our own works.

The Eternal Peace

Believers, ask yourselves honestly: Have you shared your testimony with a nonbeliever in the last week, month, or year? If not, why not? We are not spiritual sleeper cells waiting for an encrypted code word. The time is now!

I believe it is fair to deduce from Matthew chapter 24 that Jesus was offering a glimpse into our present day, a time of great deception and global uncertainty. The prophecy spoke of an age defined by political chaos, nations opposing nations, the scourge of pestilence, and the tremor of the earth beneath our feet. These global disturbances are not the finale, but rather the initial spasms of a deeper shift. For believers, the widespread evidence of these phenomena should serve as a powerful beacon of hope, affirming God's larger plan rather than provoking despair.

Our final directive is to make disciples of all nations. Therefore, our litmus test must be simple: When considering debate or protest in the name of God, pause and consider your actions. Will they lead the lost to know Jesus as their Savior, or will they sow the seeds of discontent and further drive them away? Trust that God will defend Himself according to His own plan. Paul declares, in reference to God, "*And he is not served by human hands, as if he needed anything. Rather, he himself gives everyone life and breath and everything else*" (Acts 17:25 NIV).

The ultimate answer to "Why Jesus?" is found in the eternal peace He grants:

> *Rejoice in the Lord always; again I will say, rejoice. Let your reasonableness be known to everyone. The Lord is at hand; do not be anxious about anything, but in everything by prayer and supplication with thanksgiving let your requests be made known to God. And the peace of God, which surpasses all understanding, will guard your hearts and your minds in Christ Jesus.*
>
> —Philippians 4:4–7 ESV

Through our salvation in Jesus Christ, we have gained that peace that surpasses all human understanding. Let this light of Christ shine brightly so that a lost world may see it, desire it, and come to believe in Him. In all matters and circumstances, rejoice in the Lord.

Nineteen:

DEATH, LIFE, AND THE BEGINNING OF SORROWS: WHY JESUS IS THE ANSWER

We are eternal beings, created by God, and we seek answers because we experience a void within ourselves that cannot be filled with material things or busy careers. All people hunger for a fulfilling relationship with God, whether we realize it or not.

We have examined the necessity of conviction and confronted the intellectual arguments of skepticism. Now we must turn to the ultimate point of faith—the death and resurrection of

Jesus Christ—and anchor this eternal truth to the very real and immediate anxieties of the world we inhabit today.

The Hope in Repose

A few years ago, while visiting a New York museum, I found myself completely engrossed in an early 1700s *Pietà* by the Italian sculptor Soldani. The representation captured a singular moment in history: Jesus, portrayed in repose after the crucifixion, with a mourning angel at His head and another at His feet. The latter angel, however, was not weeping; its hand was raised, signaling the coming resurrection.

I stood there, silently moved to tears, as this image brought the full scope of the gospel into focus. It was the most complete visualization of hope: Christ, in death, yet still in life, the resurrection.

Through His great suffering and ultimate sacrifice—the shedding of His pure, innocent blood for our sinful lives—He conquered sin and death once and for all. This is the promise that allows us to be redeemed in the eyes of God, living not under the shadow of judgment, but in the light of grace.

Signs of an Unsettled World

Contrast that image of ultimate hope with the world we have witnessed over the past few years. Who could have imagined a global society in total lockdown as a deadly virus ran rampant, or the widespread civil unrest and anger related to race and authority? Today, we live with deep uncertainty, filled with fear, and seemingly without hope. Many are wondering whether this is the end times the Bible warns about.

Jesus Himself spoke clearly to this concern when His disciples asked about the signs of His coming. As He sat upon the Mount of Olives, they asked Him privately:

> *Tell us, when shall these things be? and what shall be the sign of thy coming, and of the end of the world? And Jesus answered and said unto them, Take heed that no man deceive you. For many shall come in my name, saying, I am Christ; and shall deceive many. And ye shall hear of wars and rumours of wars: see that ye be not troubled: for all these things must come to pass, but the end is not yet. For nation shall rise against nation, and kingdom against kingdom: and there shall be famines, and pestilences, and earthquakes, in divers places. All these are the beginning of sorrows.*
>
> —Matthew 24:3–8

Jesus's response serves as both a warning and a source of assurance. Given these signs, our inevitable mortality feels more immediate than ever. Are you fearful? Do you feel anxious considering the chaos that points towards the return of Christ? You don't have to be. We have answers that can free the heart from anxiety, regardless of how close we are to the end.

The Dangerous Comfort of Self-Made Religion

The question we face is not *if* we will die, but what happens after death? Does this brief period on earth comprise all that there is? Do we simply return to the earth as debris, or is there something more? Most people spend their lives avoiding this question or trying to work out the answer in their own minds. The common, self-created god usually adheres to a simple, comforting idea: "I believe in a higher being that loves us, and when we die, we go on to a better place."

This is a dangerous approach to a question that impacts on our eternal life. By taking this path of least resistance, many settle the issue without having to dive into the necessary weeds of spiritual life. It's tempting to take the easy way out and simply say that we pass on to a better place.

Honestly, to a certain degree, I understand why people retreat. So many that I speak with are put off by the modern-day church in America. It has, over the last seventy years, become more of a club than a committed outreach to the masses. And the message of eternal life—the good news of the gospel—has been lost in the shuffle. Yet, the failing of modern institutions does not negate the power of the eternal truth.

I sometimes wonder if churches are evolving not to please God, but rather to soothe their own congregants or to appear familiar and comfortable to the passing visitor. This was brought into sharp focus by a recent discussion I had with a person new to the faith. He had decided to give church a try, yet what he shared was both heartfelt and deeply concerning regarding the current state of worship.

He confessed that he had reached a point of spiritual hunger, realizing the thing missing from his life was a relationship with God. With a high level of eagerness and anticipation, he expected to walk through the church doors and experience a reverent atmosphere of worship, a sanctified space unlike anything he encountered on the outside. While he expressed a profound joy that he was growing closer to the Lord, he shared a deep sense of disappointment that the church's atmosphere felt too comfortable, too familiar, like lingering in a coffee shop or gathering in a shopping mall food court.

His observation cuts to the heart of the matter: He didn't want the church to reflect the world he was trying to leave behind; he wanted it to be different. And isn't that how it should be? The sanctuary should not mirror secular culture in its effort to appear "relevant." When we commit to serving the Lord daily and placing Christ above all things, our life naturally reflects this difference, a distinction that is spiritual, not stylistic. The love and transforming power of Jesus will shine through in all manners of conduct, but this difference must begin with the reverence we show Him in worship.

We are eternal beings, created by God, and we seek answers because we experience a void within ourselves that cannot be filled with material things or busy careers. All people hunger for a fulfilling relationship with God, whether we realize it or not.

In this journey, we must heed the Apostle Paul's warnings in his writings to Timothy where he speaks of those who will create their own forms of religion, holding to a "form of godliness" but denying the power of God. Paul warns us to avoid such people and beliefs, for the danger puts those who embrace them at risk of losing everything in eternity.

One Step of Faith

Every person has the opportunity to reconcile with God through our Savior, Jesus Christ. This process requires humility, putting aside our own pride and self-sufficiency. We must acknowledge our separation from God due to our sins and transgressions before we can accept the gift of salvation.

God does not blame us for existing in this fallen world, but because God is perfection, He cannot dwell with us unless we are redeemed. This is why He gave His Son, Jesus Christ—God in the flesh—as a sacrifice so that we could be made new. This ultimate sacrifice is the gift that brings us into that close relationship with our Creator, which was intended from the beginning.

The message of hope is this: You are of great value in the sight of God, our Creator. It doesn't matter what you've done; God's love is there for you. This eternal relationship, made possible through Christ, bridges the gap that stands between us and our heavenly Father.

Simply through your one step of faith, believing that Christ died for you and was resurrected by God, that relationship with our Creator is fulfilled. Do you believe in Jesus Christ? Have you taken the time to think it over?

> *Behold, I stand at the door, and knock: if any man hear my voice, and open the door, I will come in to him.*
>
> —Revelation 3:20

The Truth That Changed Peter

To understand the transformative power of the resurrection, we need only look at the example of the Apostle Peter. Jesus chose twelve disciples as His first followers. They saw miracle upon miracle—the blind made to see, the lame healed, even the dead returned to life. Yet, when Jesus was arrested and led away to the cross, Peter, one of the boldest, denied three times that he even knew Christ. In those days leading up to the crucifixion, Peter cowered in fear for his own life.

What happened after the crucifixion to bring about a radical change in Peter? What enabled him to go on to establish the early church and lead thousands to know Christ? Peter saw the resurrected Christ.

It was the miracle of the resurrection on that third day that changed Peter forever. He was no longer motivated by fear, but by absolute conviction. He went on to preach the good news, to lead the new church, and eventually, when the Roman Emperor Nero had him arrested, no longer cowering in fear for his own life, Peter stood firm in the truth. He had witnessed the death on the cross and the life in the resurrection. Peter's faith as one of hundreds of eyewitnesses to the resurrected Christ, was the foundation upon which he boldly stood, no longer denying Christ but establishing the church right up until the very end—even unto death by crucifixion.

At Easter, we celebrate the confirmation of God's eternal plan to rescue mankind from the clutches of our enemy through the death and the life of our Savior, Jesus Christ. The resurrection confirms "*the way, the truth and the life*" of which Jesus described Himself. This path upon which we all traverse brings us to the crossroads and the decision that everyone must address. Which path will you choose for all eternity? Will you choose the broad path that leads to destruction or the narrow way that leads to eternal life with Christ?

> *If you declare with your mouth, "Jesus as Lord," and believe in your heart that God raised him from the dead, you will be saved. For it is with your heart that you believe and are justified, and it is with your mouth that you profess your faith and are saved.*
>
> —Romans 10:9–10 NIV

You can be released from a life of fear and uncertainty. All you have to do is take that first step of faith and accept the truth: Jesus is the true Son of God, and He gave His life as a ransom payment for your sins. You don't have to do anything else, because you can't earn this gift from our loving

God. As Paul tells us in Galatians 2:21, "*I do not set aside the grace of God, for if righteousness could be gained through the law, Christ died for nothing*" (NIV)!" Do you know Jesus?

An Invitation to Believe

We have detailed the signs of the times, showing how the world finds itself teetering at the precipice of the "*beginning of sorrows.*" Yet, even as time rushes onward and worldly comforts fail to satisfy the deepest spiritual hunger, this remains true: In the eyes of God, your Creator, you have intrinsic, immeasurable value.

As I have expressed throughout this book, God is absolute love, and He wills that none should perish, desiring instead that all will come to redemption through Jesus the Messiah. The invitation is not just for tomorrow or for some distant, more convenient moment. It is for right now, today.

I sincerely urge you to take that step of faith and accept the gift of salvation before this opportunity expires. Please don't let this moment pass; you may never have this clarity, this chance, again. Remember the inevitability of the path ahead: In one moment, your time will expire, and you will stand before your Creator. Will you be ready?

Twenty:

THE FOUNDATION OF FAITH: TRUST AND OBEY

> *"Trust in the Lord with all your heart and lean not on your own understanding; in all your ways submit to him, and he will make your paths straight."*
>
> —Proverbs 3:5–6 NIV

If the resurrection is the ultimate declaration of hope, then faith is the bedrock upon which that hope stands. It is the active, deliberate choice to accept that God's plan is superior to our own logic, especially when our circumstances look bleakest. This entire concept is wrapped up perfectly in one of the most beloved wisdom verses in Scripture: "*Trust in the*

Lord with all your heart and lean not on your own understanding; in all your ways submit to him, and he will make your paths straight" (Proverbs 3:5–6 NIV).

Growing up in a Southern Baptist church, I have fond memories of the old classic hymns we'd sing every Sunday morning. One had this familiar chorus: "Trust and obey, for there's no other way, to be happy in Jesus, but to trust and obey." This simple refrain holds a decisive and profound truth that Christ taught throughout His earthly ministry.

Defining the Substance of Hope

The Bible gives us a clear definition of what the essential foundation of faith is all about: "*Now faith is the substance of things hoped for, the evidence of things not seen*" (Hebrews 11:1). We are certainly called to pray in faithfulness, seeking God's direction and guidance in all things. When we are troubled or facing deep uncertainty, we instinctively turn to our heavenly Father for help.

But the real question is not whether we reach out, but how we reach out. Do we truly know how to petition the Lord in genuine faith? Do we lay our burdens before Him and then unconditionally trust Him to work things out for the best, according to His will, not our meticulously crafted, expected outcome?

Over the years, I've learned valuable and sometimes painful lessons about this dynamic. I confess I have failed many times in my own approach to God. When I was younger in the faith, I would pray for certain needs and requests, and then, because I was unwilling to wait and truly exercise my faith, I would begin meddling in the expected outcome. By rushing ahead of God's perfect timing, I spoiled the opportunity to grow my trust and receive God's very best for my life.

Our human tendency is to reason things out, try to fix them, and maintain control. We are limited, viewing each situation through a narrow keyhole of experience and understanding. God, however, is all-knowing, all-powerful, and He is always at work toward the absolute best results according to His eternal plans. Often, we come to Him with a facade of faith, yet we bring our own solutions in hand. We try to place our requests before Him while dictating the logical, desired outcomes that make sense to our finite minds. This approach is not faith at all; it is the very definition of leaning on our own understanding, a trap that keeps us from witnessing the spectacular things God wants to do.

The Perfect Example of Obedience

The single greatest example we can observe regarding perfect prayer, faith, and accepting God's perfect will comes from Jesus Christ Himself. The hour was fast approaching for His betrayal and subsequent crucifixion. In the Garden of Gethsemane, we see in excruciating detail the proper way to petition our heavenly Father.

> *Then Jesus came with them to a place called Gethsemane, and he told the disciples, "Sit here while I go over there and pray." Taking along Peter and the two sons of Zebedee, he began to be sorrowful and troubled. He said to them, "**I am deeply grieved to the point of death.** Remain here and stay awake with me." Going a little farther, he fell facedown and prayed, "**My Father, if it is possible, let this cup pass from me. Yet not as I will, but as you will.**"'*
>
> —Matthew 26:36–39 CSB (emphasis added)

Jesus was facing the darkest hours of His time on earth; the weight of the world's sin was about to be laid upon Him. Yet, knowing God's plan and trusting in the Father's unfailing wisdom, He sought not His own will, but the perfect will of God. He was so deeply grieved that He fell face down in prayer. Imagine that point of grief. We all have times when we are afraid, when we've lost a job or when we face great uncertainty. At that point, we turn to God, earnestly seeking help from the storms of life.

It is then that our faith is truly tested. Through these trials, we grow, but that requires patience through faith, placing our needs at His feet and then trusting and waiting on God's perfect timing to deliver us according to His will. If God immediately solved every problem we face, we would not need faith, and we would never grow. It is through our deliverance that our testimony is strengthened and becomes useful in sustaining other believers.

When we approach God with this level of surrendered trust, we receive a peace that transcends our difficulties. As the Apostle Paul wrote:

> *Don't worry about anything, but in everything, through prayer and petition with thanksgiving, present your requests to God. And the peace of God, which surpasses all understanding, will guard your hearts and minds in Christ Jesus.*
>
> —Philippians 4:6–7 CSB

The Danger of Human Concerns

A very important part of the faith process is allowing God room to work things out according to His purposes. Often, we come to God in faith, but we bring our own solutions. We see this human limitation perfectly demonstrated in the example of Peter.

Peter, the strong voice who believed in Christ with all his heart, was the one who proclaimed: "*You are the Messiah, the Son of the living God.*" Yet, we also see this well-intended Peter fail to understand God's perfect plan of redemption.

After Jesus shared with the disciples the necessity of His coming persecution, death, and resurrection, Peter was unwilling to accept it. He had given up everything to follow Christ and could not reason out in his own mind that he would have to watch Jesus die. He was bound by his own small view of the world, thus remaining blind to the greater works of God.

We see in hindsight why these things had to happen, but Peter was in the moment, just as we are when we face difficulties and tragedies. We must learn from this lesson and put aside our own reasoning by trusting in God, knowing that His plan is perfect and His timing is for our ultimate benefit. Peter suffered a terrible rebuke from Jesus for his failure to trust God's plan:

> *From then on Jesus began to point out to his disciples that it was necessary for him to go to Jerusalem and suffer many things . . . be killed, and be raised the third day. Peter took him aside and began to rebuke him, "Oh no, Lord! This will never happen to you!" Jesus turned and told Peter, "**Get behind me, Satan! You are a hindrance to me because you're not thinking about God's concerns but human concerns.**"*
>
> —Matthew 16:21–23 CSB (emphasis added)

Peter's attempt to save Jesus was a hindrance to the plan of salvation for all mankind. This should make us pause and ask ourselves: In our prayers for ourselves and others, are we advocating for God's perfect will or merely our own human desires and outcomes?

How Does Faith Grow?

So, where do believers go to grow in their faith? Where does that trust begin? "*So then faith cometh by hearing, and hearing by the word of God*" (Romans 10:17). We must strive to know God better each day, and the way to grow in knowledge and faith is through the study of the Word of God. From His Word, we learn to understand and trust in God's will for our lives and the lives of others.

When someone needs prayer for illness, we always go first to the request for healing. But what about praying for the afflicted to remain faithful, humble, and steadfast in their commitment to the Lord? We may pray for immediate healing, but God may have other, greater plans for that person's life and their testimony. It's not wrong to pray for healing, but in this and all situations, we should strive to put aside our own reasoning and know that God is working all things for the good for those who are called by His name.

This deep, abiding trust in the Lord—this faith—is the bridge that connects the anxiety of the "beginning of sorrows" with the peace promised by the risen Christ.

Twenty-One:

THE *PARAKLETOS*: POWER TO TRUST, STRENGTH TO CONSOLE

If we choose to live by the Spirit, the outward manifestation of that power is clear and transformative. Instead of the works of the flesh (like hatred, strife, and envy), our lives produce a constant harvest of divine character.

We have settled the issue of salvation through the death and resurrection of Jesus Christ, and we have committed to the foundation of faith—to trust in God's will above our own human understanding. But how, exactly, do we achieve that level of sustained, surrendered trust? How do we access the patience and wisdom needed to stop leaning on our own limited reasoning, especially when the sorrows of life press in? The answer lies in the third person of the Holy Trinity: The Holy Spirit.

When Jesus left the earth, He did not leave us as orphans to face the beginning of sorrows alone. He promised to send a powerful, divine presence who would serve as our living connection to God. In the original Greek, this helper is called the *Parakletos*.

The Parakletos: One Called to Our Side

The word *parakletos* is richly layered, but its core meaning is "one who is called to one's side to help." It describes a relationship that is active, intimate, and immediately available. Jesus promised that the Holy Spirit would be a comforter, advocate, and helper who would provide peace, solace, strength, hope, encouragement, and assurance to believers in times of need; he would also enable us to console others.

This concept is key to understanding our life as believers. We are not saved to live an isolated existence; we are saved into a relationship with our Creator, sustained by the Spirit who is always with us, ready to guide us.

We acknowledge here the foundational truth of the Holy Trinity: the perfect union of God the Father (the source and planner), God the Son (Jesus Christ, the redeemer and the way), and God the Holy Spirit (the active, comforting presence who indwells believers and executes God's will on earth).

The Role of Our Advocate and Guide

The Holy Spirit serves several critical roles that enable us to live out the radical trust we discussed in the last chapter:

- **The Divine Teacher (Advocate).** The Spirit is not just a passive feeling; He is an active instructor, guiding us into a deeper relationship with God and understanding of scripture. Jesus said:

  But the Comforter, which is the Holy Ghost, whom the Father will send in my name, he shall teach you all things, and bring all things to your remembrance, whatsoever I have said unto you (John 14:26).

  This means that when you are troubled and turn to God, the Spirit is there to teach you how to pray according to God's will and advocate on your behalf. He reminds you of the truths of Scripture, so you don't have to lean solely on your flawed human memory or reasoning.

- **The Guide to All Truth (Source of Strength).** When we face confusion, the Holy Spirit acts as our definitive guide, ensuring we stay focused on God's eternal plan rather than getting pulled aside by "human concerns," as Peter did.

> *Howbeit when he, the Spirit of truth, is come, he will guide you into all truth: for he shall not speak of himself; but whatsoever he shall hear, that shall he speak: and he will shew you things to come* (John 16:13).

The Spirit provides the necessary strength and discernment to navigate the complex, unsettling realities of our modern world. When the news or the pandemic or civil unrest makes you fearful, the Spirit guides you back to the perfect truth of God's sovereignty. He is your Consoler, replacing anxiety with His peace.

- **The Power to Console Others.** Because the Spirit indwells us, filling us with peace and grace, we become conduits of that same strength for the world around us. Having been comforted by the *Parakletos*, we gain the ability to console others who are walking through their own storms. Discipleship in action means allowing the Spirit to use your testimony and life to demonstrate God's faithfulness.

The Warning and the Fruit

The power of the Holy Spirit is a gift, but it is one that requires our conscious cooperation. The Spirit operates freely, but He will not override our own free will. This leads to a serious warning the Apostle Paul gave to the church in Ephesus: "*And grieve not the holy Spirit of God, whereby ye are sealed unto the day of redemption*" (Ephesians 4:30).

To grieve the Spirit means to actively bring sorrow to Him by the way you choose to live. It is not about minor missteps, but about persistent, willful unrighteousness—allowing bitterness, wrath, anger, slander, and malice to control your actions. By choosing to live according to the fallen human nature (the flesh) rather than submitting to the Spirit's guidance, we put distance between ourselves and the power we need to survive.

If we choose to live by the Spirit, the outward manifestation of that power is clear and transformative. Instead of the works of the flesh (like hatred, strife, and envy), our lives produce a constant harvest of divine character. "*But the fruit of the Spirit is love, joy, peace, longsuffering, gentleness, goodness, faith, meekness, temperance: against such there is no law*" (Galatians 5:22–23).

This is the evidence that God's Holy Spirit is working through you. This love replaces anger; this peace replaces fear. This is how we know we are truly resting in God's will and not our own. The Christian life is not a struggle to earn these traits, but simply an act of allowing the Spirit, already dwelling within, to express Himself through us. Our mandate, therefore, is clear: "*If we live in the Spirit, let us also walk in the Spirit*" (Galatians 5:25).

This is the key to activating the trust we discussed. If you've accepted Christ, the Spirit is present. Now, simply choose to walk—to live, act, and reason—by His direction, and you will find the strength to trust the Lord with all your heart, no matter what sorrows may come.

Twenty-Two:

THE DAILY WALK: ENGAGING THE SPIRIT THROUGH WORD AND PRAYER

Prayer is the crucial step of laying our will down and saying, "Not as I will, but as you will," just as Jesus modeled in Gethsemane.

We've established that faith is the foundation of our trust, and the Holy Spirit (the *Parakletos*) is the divine power who enables that trust. The Spirit is not a distant force; He is an active, indwelling presence ready to guide us. The central question then becomes: How do we practically engage this divine Helper in the routine, messy, and demanding rhythm of our daily lives?

The Spirit's power is accessed and amplified through two primary, inseparable disciplines that must define the life of every true believer: the study of God's Word and prayer.

The Two Pillars of Engagement

- **The Word: The Spirit's Textbook.** If we are to succeed at the command to "*lean not on your own understanding*," we must replace our limited human wisdom with God's perfect wisdom. The Holy Spirit accomplishes this primarily through the Word of God.

  Remember the simple truth: "*faith cometh by hearing, and hearing by the word of God*" (Romans 10:17). You cannot trust someone you do not know, and you cannot know God without consistently studying the revelation He gave us of Himself.

  The Bible is the Spirit's textbook. As the divine teacher (John 14:26), the Holy Spirit uses the Scripture to do several things in our daily walk:

  - **He Corrects Our Thinking:** When we feel fear, He reminds us of promises of peace. When we are tempted to manipulate an outcome He uses the Word to correct our short-sighted, human reasoning.

- › **He Provides Discernment:** The Spirit guides us into all truth (John 16:13). By consistently engaging with the Word, we build an internal filter that allows us to distinguish between God's voice and the loud, confusing static of the world.
- › **He Equips Our Testimony:** The more God's Word saturates our minds, the more the fruit of the Spirit (love, joy, peace, etc.) is manifested in our words, making our daily interactions a compelling witness to the unbelieving world.

- **Prayer: The Practice of Submission**. If Bible study is how we hear God, then prayer is how we respond and commit to obedience. Prayer is the crucial step of laying our will down and saying, "*Not as I will, but as you will,*" just as Jesus modeled in Gethsemane.

To practically engage the Spirit in prayer, we must shift our focus:

- › **From Petition to Listening.** True prayer is a conversation, not a one-sided presentation of demands. After presenting our requests "*with thanksgiving*" (Philippians 4:6), we must be patient and silent, allowing the Spirit to bring the peace that surpasses all understanding. This is where we receive the Parakletos's counsel.

- **From Solutions to Surrender.** Instead of bringing God our problem *and* our expected solution, we lay the entire situation at His feet, fully trusting that His plan is the best plan—even if it seems illogical or inconvenient to us. This moment of surrender is the highest form of trust.

The Believer's Identity: An Heir, Not an Owner

The life of a true believer is founded in faith by the immeasurable grace of God. We are saved, not by our works, but by His unmerited favor. This grace defines our identity and, crucially, our relationship with this physical world.

We must constantly explore and remind ourselves that we are only here on this earth for a short time. Scripture is explicit: our life is but a fleeting thing. "*What is your life? For you are a mist that appears for a little while and then vanishes*" (James 4:14 NIV). We are like a vapor that quickly vanishes. This realization changes everything. If our life here is temporary, then the things we obsess over—our jobs, status, possessions, and even our most intense sorrows - are also temporary in the grand scheme of eternity.

As believers, we are fundamentally not of this world. Christ Himself said to His disciples, "*I have chosen you out of the world*" (John 15:19). We are simply sojourners, ambassadors, and foreigners passing through. Our citizenship, our focus, and our inheritance are elsewhere. We are heirs to God's Kingdom. This eternal perspective is the true source of peace in the face of temporary tragedy. Why fear loss when you own the infinite?

The Calling: Shining the Light

This new identity—founded in grace, empowered by the Spirit, and focused on eternity—comes with a nonnegotiable calling: to share our faith and live as a Christlike example for the world to see.

If we know that we are merely traveling through this dark and confused world, our mission is to shine the light in the darkness around us. Our actions, our patience, our love, and our peace must stand in sharp contrast to the fear, anger, and anxiety that grip those who lean on their own understanding. "*In the same way, let your light shine before others, so that they may see your good works and give glory to your Father in heaven*" (Matthew 5:16 NIV).

When we consistently engage with God through study of the Word and prayer, we naturally produce the fruit of the Spirit (Galatians 5:22–23). The fruit of the Spirit is the visible evidence that the perfect union of the Holy Trinity is at work in our lives. It is the only testimony the world truly understands. Our life is not about fixing the world but about witnessing for the King who has already redeemed it.

Question for the Believer

Living by the Spirit is not a destination, but a daily choice to walk in Him (Galatians 5:25). As you continue your journey, which aspect of the believer's calling—witnessing through good works or actively sharing your testimony—feels more urgent for you?

Question for the Nonbeliever

In recent chapters, we addressed many of the questions that nonbelievers typically raise, and we covered the life, death, and resurrection of Jesus. We also discussed the love of our heavenly Father, which is why He sent Christ to die for our sins while we were yet sinners. Do you feel a tugging at your heart to consider inviting Jesus into your life?

Jesus tells us in Revelation chapter 3 that He stands at the door and knocks. He also promises this truth: Seek and you will find Him, ask and the door will be opened unto you. Today you can take that single step of faith and ask Christ into your heart, but as you will see in the next section, time is short.

Twenty-Three:

THE CROSSROADS: LOOK TO THE CROSS; TIME IS SHORT

Jesus gave His life and paid our debt that we could never pay. His way is never forced. The gift is there for anyone to receive without conditions, but you must answer the door and open your heart.

We have learned that the Holy Spirit provides the power for us to trust in God, even when the world around us descends into chaos. Yet, the reality we face today requires more than just internal strength; it requires a profound sense of urgency. This chapter speaks directly to two crucial truths: the undeniable signs of the times and the immediate, free path to redemption available to anyone at the crossroads of life.

The Urgency of the Hour

For anyone searching for answers, or for those who claim belief in a higher power but have yet to accept Jesus as the true Messiah, this is your warning. The time for apathy is over. The words of prophecy are no longer merely things to be studied; they are now a living example playing out for us to see with our own eyes in our world today.

- **The Signs Are All Around Us.** When the disciples asked Jesus what signs would indicate His pending return and the end of the world, He gave a clear, multi-faceted answer:

  And ye shall hear of wars and rumours of wars: see that ye be not troubled: for all these things must come to pass, but the end is not yet. For nation shall rise against nation, and kingdom against kingdom: and there shall be famines, and pestilences, and earthquakes, in divers places. All these are the beginning of sorrows.

  —Matthew 24:6–8

  These very signs—escalating wars, pestilences (global sickness and disease), and increasing desperation—are prevalent right now. Jesus did not tell the disciples that once these things started there would be any turning back. No election, no human governance, and no technology will solve these issues; this path goes above and beyond the world as we know it. The battle of good versus evil is now playing out in real-time, and we must take our stand.

To ignore this reality or choose to live in denial is the same as denying the very existence of God and our Savior Jesus Christ. You must choose a side, and the cost of the wrong decision is eternal.

- **The Final Warning.** Time is short, and there will soon come a moment when you will no longer be given the opportunity to seek the gift of salvation that comes through Jesus Christ. Jesus made the stakes perfectly clear:

  Therefore, everyone who will acknowledge me before others, I will also acknowledge him before my Father in heaven. But whoever denies me before others, I will also deny him before my Father in heaven.

  —Matthew 10:32–33 CSB

  Do not wait until it's too late. Consider making that step of faith today, right now, by asking Jesus to forgive you of your sins and welcoming Him into your heart. Remember the simple but brutal truth: the wages of sin is death.

Quiet Desperation and True Hope

In a world defined by self-reliance, the consequences of a life without eternal meaning are tragically clear. As the playwright Arthur Miller's character, Willy Loman, observed in *Death of a Salesman*: "Funny, y'know? After all the highways, and the trains, and the appointments, and the years, you end up worth more dead than alive."[23] And Henry David Thoreau grimly stated that "The mass of men lead lives of quiet desperation."[24]

Where is hope? Today we see despair and outright desperation as people are losing any hope of a better tomorrow. Do we truly work and toil our entire lives only to end up worth more dead than alive? Sadly, in the godless world, the answer is yes. However, we are not forsaken. We are not without hope.

The Crossroads Is the Cross

For those facing a crossroads, feeling the quiet desperation, and sensing the hopelessness of the world's systems, your answer is not in better politics or greater technology. It is found in one place: look to the cross. The ultimate

---

[23] Arthur Miller, *Death of a Salesman* (Penguin Classics, 2000), 76.

[24] Henry David Thoreau, *Walden, or Life in the Woods* (Vintage Books, 1991), 43.

confirmation of God's love and the availability of grace is found in the scene of Christ's suffering:

> *One of the criminals who hung there hurled insults at him: "Aren't you the Messiah? Save yourself and us!" But the other criminal rebuked him. "Don't you fear God," he said, "since you are under the same sentence? We are punished justly, for we are getting what our deeds deserve. But this man has done nothing wrong." Then he said, "Jesus, remember me when you come into your kingdom." Jesus answered him, "Truly I tell you, today you will be with me in paradise."*
>
> —Luke 23:39–43 NIV

This profound moment demonstrates the perfection of God's love for all mankind. It is the entirety of the gospel message—the good news—as it validates the availability of redemption to anyone and everyone without exception.

- **Acknowledge Your Guilt:** The thief first confessed, "*We are punished justly, for we are getting what our deeds deserve.*" This is the essential first step: acknowledging your own sin and the debt you owe.
- **Profess Your Faith:** The thief then declared, "*Jesus, remember me when you come into your kingdom.*" In that one lucid pronouncement, he

professed faith while acknowledging Jesus as the Son of God, the Messiah.

- **Receive God's Grace:** Jesus's response, "*Truly I tell you, today you will be with me in paradise*" is the answer to our quiet desperation. No additional requirements were placed upon the thief; Jesus extended God's perfect, unconditional grace upon his entire being.

Choose Life

Today, many are placing their faith in governments and man-made institutions. They claim to seek love and inclusion, yet their actions display division and exclusion because the world does not know truth, having rejected the One who is truth. If you cannot understand truth, you can never demonstrate true love. The battle is not against human systems, but against a greater, spiritual evil:

> *For our struggle is not against flesh and blood, but against the rulers, against the authorities, against the powers of this dark world and against the spiritual forces of evil in the heavenly realms.*
>
> —Ephesians 6:12 NIV

Governments claim to have solutions that are forced upon their subjects. But Jesus offers the one true path of freedom and peace. "*Behold, I stand at the door and knock.*

If anyone hears my voice and opens the door, I will come in to him and dine with him, and he with me" (Revelation 3:20 ESV).

Jesus gave His life and paid our debt that we could never pay. His way is never forced. The gift is there for anyone to receive, without conditions, but you must answer the door and open your heart. The world has reached a crossroads. Does one advance along the broad path that leads to destruction or take up the narrow path toward redemption? This choice weighs eternal upon every soul.

Questions for Reflection:

- Where do you find yourself today? Are you living a life of quiet desperation or a life of peace beyond human understanding?
- What is the one thing you are still relying on for security instead of Jesus Christ?

Twenty-Four:

THE POWER OF THE PARDON: FORGIVENESS AND THE CALL TO COMMUNITY

With profound, unmerited grace comes a radical responsibility: We must also forgive those who have wronged us.

The central theme of Christianity is forgiveness, and this single truth is what sets the Christian faith apart from every other religious system on earth. All other religions are built on a foundation of human effort—what *we* must do to please the divine—but Christianity rests entirely on the foundation of God's finished work through the substitutionary sacrifice of Jesus Christ.

The Unearned Gift: Christ's Complete Work

The beautiful and essential paradox of the gospel is this: We can do nothing of our own accord to gain forgiveness; it is a gift from God.

God, being perfectly holy, cannot tolerate sin. The debt for our rebellion (sin) is spiritual death, a price we were incapable of paying. Therefore, God sent His only Son, Jesus, who lived a life without blemish. He voluntarily gave His life, the Lamb to the slaughter, to pay that price in our place through His death and resurrection.

> *Otherwise, Christ would have had to suffer many times since the creation of the world. But he has appeared once for all at the culmination of the ages to do away with sin by the sacrifice of himself.*
>
> —Hebrews 9:26 NIV

This declaration of faith, by the Grace of God, secures our salvation.

The Security of Salvation

One of the greatest truths of the Bible is that Christ died for all our sins, not just some, but all of them: past, present, and future. "*And this is the testimony: God has given us eternal life, and this life is in his Son. Whoever has the Son has life; whoever does not have the Son of God does not have life*" (1 John 5:11–12 NIV).

This means we don't lose our salvation every time we sin, otherwise, we would lose it daily. Our salvation is eternally secured in the person of Christ, not in the perfection of our performance.

The Call to Forgive Others

With this profound, unmerited grace comes a radical responsibility: We must also forgive those who have wronged us. The moment we accept God's forgiveness; we are called to embody that same grace toward others. This is often the most difficult daily discipline because it is not about feelings and emotions; it is a tangible act of will, driven by the logic of the cross. How can we withhold a pardon from another when we have received the ultimate pardon ourselves?

Writhing in pain, slowly bleeding out from the beating he had received, hanging on that rugged cross, while people mocked him and divided his belongings among themselves, Jesus looked down upon them with compassion as He asked God, "*Father, forgive them, for they know not what they do*" (Luke 23:34 ESV).

Forgiving someone doesn't mean forgetting the injury or pretending it didn't happen. It means surrendering the right to seek revenge or hold them in a prison of debt. It is a necessary step that frees us from the burden of bitterness, allowing the Spirit to bring peace to the soul.

Holiness and the Spirit

Though our salvation is secure, this security is not a license to sin at will. Sin is serious; it is an offense to a holy God. We are called to reflect the nature of the One who saved us: "*But just as he who called you is holy, so be holy in all you do; for it is written: 'Be holy, because I am holy*'" (1 Peter 1:15–16 NIV).

As we discussed in the previous chapter, we can't live a Christian life on our own strength. We need the Holy Spirit (the *Parakletos*) to provide the power to choose holiness over sin. It is the Spirit who convicts us when we stumble and guides us toward repentance. We are also called to be a witness to the wonders of God and the blessed hope we have through Christ Jesus our Lord.

Public Declaration: The Meaning of Baptism

Following our private proclamation of faith, we are called to follow in Jesus's own example of baptism. It is vital to understand that baptism is not a requirement for salvation. We know this because salvation stands on its own, as displayed by the thief on the cross. He expressed his faith in Jesus as the Messiah, acknowledged his guilt, and yet, not having the opportunity for baptism, Jesus proclaimed: "*Truly I tell you, today you will be with me in paradise.*" We are saved by grace through faith.

However, baptism is an important step that we should take to publicly identify ourselves with Christ. It is an act of obedience to God and a way to publicly declare our decision to follow Christ. Baptism is a sign of our new life:

1. **Burial:** We are submersed in water, symbolically dying to our old, sinful self.
2. **Cleansing:** We are washed clean by the blood of Jesus shed on the cross.
3. **Resurrection:** We rise from the water a new creation in our faith in Christ.

As the evangelist Billy Graham preached, "Baptism is a conclusive act of obedience and witness to the world that we are Christ's."[25]

Questions for Consideration:

- **For the Believer:** Is there someone you need to forgive today? Take a moment to surrender that hurt to God and release the debt, not based on your feelings, but on the grace you have received.
- **For the Seeker:** Do you still believe there is something you must *do* (a work, a ritual, or an act) to be made right with God, or have you accepted

---

[25] Billy Graham, "Basics of Christianity—Baptism," Billy Graham Evangelistic Association, accessed January 12, 2026, https://billygraham.org/basics-of-christianity/baptism.

that His forgiveness is a gift through Jesus Christ alone?

- **For All:** If you have accepted Christ, have you taken the step of baptism to publicly acknowledge your commitment to Him?

Twenty-Five:

THE CROSSROADS OF CALVARY: THE JUDGMENT AND THE CHOICE

Jesus has paid our debt of sin through His death and resurrection; you simply must make the choice to follow Him. If not, you will pay the wages of your sin, which is death, eternal separation from God.

The scene is Golgotha, the "Place of the Skull," known in Latin as Calvary. It is here, outside the city gates of Jerusalem, that the long-awaited collision between divine justice and infinite love took place. This hill became the ultimate altar, not for a burnt offering of an animal, but for the one, perfect sacrifice of the Son of God. At the center of this desolate tableau, Jesus is suspended on a cross, flanked on either side by a common criminal, each receiving their rightful punishment for crimes against the Roman Empire.

This deliberate alignment, three crosses against the sky, was no accident of history. It was the eternal crossroads by which all mankind must pass, and it stands as the final, compelling visual for the entirety of the Christian faith.

The Prophetic Foreshadowing

The prophets of the Old Testament pointed forward to Jesus, yet today many people deny the Savior and follow the broad path that leads to destruction. Over six hundred years before this crucifixion, the prophet Isaiah peered into the future and delivered the most profound summary of what would occur on that hill:

> *But he was pierced for our transgressions, he was crushed for our iniquities; the punishment that brought us peace was on him, and by his wounds we are healed. We all, like sheep, have gone astray, each of us has turned to our own way; and the Lord has laid on him the iniquity of us all.*
>
> —Isaiah 53:5–6 NIV

These are wise words and prophetic insight as we are blessed by Isaiah in his pronouncements as he points toward the Messiah. His words are a necessary reminder that we, like sheep, have gone astray as we pursue our own path in this life. We know this human condition is not accidental. The wisest of all rulers, the King of Israel, son of David, Solomon, whose reign spanned more than nine hundred years before Christ, delivers the ecclesiastical knowledge outlining the seasons of our lives:

> *There is a time for everything, and a season for every activity under the heavens: a time to be born and a time to die, a time to plant and a time to uproot, a time to kill and a time to heal, a time to tear down and a time to build, a time to weep and a time to laugh, a time to mourn and a time to dance.*
>
> —Ecclesiastes 3:1–4 NIV

Solomon goes on to show that God has set eternity in the human heart; we are not the finite gathering of organisms that accidentally discovered life only to live and die, returning to nothing. We are eternal beings designed by our Creator, yet we cannot fathom what God has done from beginning to end. However, included in this summary of life is the reminder found later in Ecclesiastes 3:15 as the final seasons pass, "*God will call the past to account.*"

From the beginning we know that God used many prophets of old to point toward the coming of Jesus. Isaiah, Moses, Jeremiah, Micah, Zechariah—and more throughout time—all shared God-given insights of hope for mankind that Jesus was coming. In beautiful contrast, the New Testament announces the good news of our Messiah's arrival: "*For God did not send his Son into the world to condemn the world, but to save the world through him*" (John 3:17 NIV).

Through this we know that God has not forsaken us in this fallen world. To the contrary, God sent Jesus into this world with one mission—to give His life as a sacrifice for all. He was crushed for our iniquities. Upon that cross, Jesus demonstrated perfect obedience to God's plan as He gave His life to atone for our sins.

The Two Thieves: A Question of Alignment

The setting of the crucifixion, with Christ positioned between two convicted thieves, offered a profound and agonizing contrast. While the criminals received their due penalty for crimes against the Roman Empire, Jesus—savagely beaten and stripped of all human dignity—was fulfilling a divine purpose. This moment, witnessed by all, reflected the full measure of God's love; it was the culmination of everything the Prophets foretold concerning the coming Messiah, and it established the very foundation of unwavering Hope that we find confirmed in God's Word.

Even in those final hours, a criminal receiving his just sentence found his way to faith. His interaction with Christ resulted not in condemnation, but in an immediate and startling guarantee of acceptance. The entire event transcends mere history; it is a timeless testament to the good news, proving the boundless and immediate accessibility of salvation for all mankind.

To one side a thief mocks him, echoing the voices of the Pharisees and the skeptical crowd. The mocking thief stands as a stark representation of those whose view of God is purely transactional, seeing the divine only as a means to an end. He embodies the consumer mentality that demands immediate rescue and material solutions to earthly problems, and then bitterly rejects and scorns God when their specific demands are not met on their own terms.

In stark contrast, the other thief models true repentance. He quietly acknowledged his own guilt, accepting his sentence with profound humility. He understood that he was being punished justly, recognizing the cosmic difference between his own deeds and the innocence of the man beside him. In one final, lucid moment of faith, he looked past the physical suffering and confessed his belief in the eternal authority of Christ, petitioning, not for immediate escape, but for remembrance in the coming kingdom. This act represents the perfect surrender to grace: the moment faith supersedes sight.

In this moment, the dying thief fulfills the simplicity of the gospel itself. This moment is candid and compelling, and it speaks to everyone no matter who you are, what your social status may be, or what you may have done. All paths lead to the cross for all of mankind, from the prophets looking forward, to modern day as we look to what Christ has done for us. The question becomes, upon which cross do we align?

Pause on this scenario for a moment: three crosses, Jesus is front and center, with one thief on each side. Understanding that every word in the Bible is purposeful; look at what this scene represents to us. Jesus has already proclaimed that He is the way, the truth, and the life. No man comes to the Father except through Him. Therefore, Jesus is presented as the sacrifice, the lamb led to the slaughter, taking our sins upon His body. The two thieves demonstrate the internal debate we must reconcile within our own being: Do we believe that Jesus is the Messiah and place our faith in Him, or do we turn away and reject Christ? We can do nothing of our own merits to secure redemption with God, it is only by the grace of God through faith in Christ that we are saved.

The Finality of the Atonement

The world is full of false doctrines and confusion, with many choosing to worship creation rather than acknowledge and worship the Creator. We see a world that has given itself over to its own selfish indulgences and, as Paul warned, people do not have a tolerance for the truth; they gather around them those that will speak what they want to hear. Many hold to a form of godliness but deny the power and deity of Christ. Some don't believe we need redemption at all, but make no mistake about it: "*For all have sinned and come short of the glory of God*" (Romans 3:23).

As we previously shared through the wise words of Solomon, God has placed eternity in our hearts. We are not finite beings and deep down we all know that to be true. There is more to life than the mundane distractions we seek from sunrise to sunset. For those who have come to that place of atonement, having called out to the Lord in faith, believing in the death and resurrection of our Savior, Jesus Christ, the heart is filled to overflowing with the peace and joy that surpasses all human understanding.

For those who ignore or reject this open offer of forgiveness, the knowledge of an eternal existence transforms into a source of constant torment—a spiritual millstone driving an endless, futile search for fulfillment. Every person, simply by being, is forced into a choice. In this manner of being, whether we want to acknowledge it or not, we must choose which side of Christ we will hang our eternal destiny.

The promise of redemption was secured when Jesus uttered his final, triumphant word from the cross: *"Tetelestai."* This Greek word is often translated as "It is finished." In the ancient world, it was used to mark a document as "Paid in Full." The debt of our sin, the infinite separation between a Holy God and sinful man, was canceled forever. To confirm this, the Gospel of Matthew records this climactic event: "*At that moment the curtain of the temple was torn in two from top to bottom*" (Matthew 27:51 NIV). The heavy veil separating the common people from the presence of God in the Holy of Holies was ripped apart, symbolizing that the way to God was now open to all, purchased by the blood of Christ.

We have the opportunity, because God does not want

that any should perish, but that all would come to Christ. But we must choose the path to our eternal destiny; putting off the decision or ignoring this reality is, in and of itself, a denial of Christ. Read this most sobering text spoken by Jesus:

> *Enter through the narrow gate. For wide is the gate and broad is the path that leads to destruction, and many enter through it. But small is the gate and narrow the path that leads to life, and few will find it* (Matthew 7:13–14 NIV).
>
> *Then he said to them all: "Whoever wants to be my disciple must deny themselves and take up their cross daily and follow me. For whoever wants to save their life will lose it, but whoever loses their life for me will save it"* (Luke 9:23–24 NIV).

Today, we stand at this very place—the eternal crossroads by which all mankind must pass. It is here that you must determine the path upon which your destiny will proceed. The choice is stark, mirroring the two men on either side of the Lord: Upon which cross will you forever nail your eternal soul? Will you follow the path of the mocking thief, demanding that Christ conform to your temporal needs, or will you humbly bow and confess your sins while professing your faith in the Savior? The two paths could not be clearer: one leads to the narrow gate that "few will find," while the other, the broad path of ease and self-reliance, leads only to eternal separation from God.

The urgency of this choice cannot be overstated. You can choose Jesus today—right here and now. Because a day is coming when God will call every aspect of our past to account. We will stand before our Creator, and the only question that matters will be the status of our debt. If you have accepted Christ into your heart, you will stand in perfect peace, because your entire account will show a zero balance—Paid in Full.

Jesus has already settled our insurmountable debt of sin through His death and victorious resurrection. Your part is not to earn it, but simply to make the choice to follow Him. If you choose to ignore or reject this payment, you will inevitably pay the wages of your sins—which is death, eternal separation from God. But the payment has been made, the offer is open, and the gate is waiting. Will you surrender your claim to self-justice and accept the perfect grace that awaits you today?

For those who have already accepted Christ, this moment is not about initial salvation, but about re-dedication. Perhaps you have allowed the daily grind, past failures, or lingering guilt to steal your passion, leaving your light dim and your fervor cold. If the weight of shame is holding you captive, hear the truth of the cross again: God bought you at a price—a price already paid, demanding nothing less than the life of His only Son. You are no longer your own; the debt is settled, and therefore, the chains of regret and inadequacy are broken. Look once more at the staggering cost of your redemption and let that love propel you forward. Right now, you are invited to leave that stagnation behind, to fully embrace your freedom, and to rededicate yourself to living as the salt and the light—a vibrant, living testimony to the saving grace and unwavering hope we find in God the Father.

Twenty-Six:

PROGRESSIVELY VULGAR – THE CULT OF THE ONE-WORLD ORDER

The socialist promise is security and equity; the communist reality is forced submission and oppression. Their initial promise of shared resources quickly devolves into God's benevolent rule being replaced with man's tyrannical control.

Our world is effectively a ship of fools, adrift and heading down the broad path that leads to destruction. We are saturated with the voices of arrogant marginalization, spoken by foolish people obsessed with their own self-importance. They leverage a moral pulpit defined by fleeting concepts of "tolerance" and "inclusion," weaponizing these ideas to divide the masses and enforce a compliance that demands nothing less than the rejection of absolute truth.

In the public forum, tolerance and inclusion are in fact neither—nothing more than convenient placeholders. They are a podium upon which the progressive elites pontificate while marginalizing individuals or groups, which they neither tolerate nor include. They steal from our language, as common thieves in a marketplace of past societal failures, taking words and phrases that imply a virtuous form of respectable traits while driving their bloody daggers deep into the moral fabric of a world created by God and inhabited by those created in His image.

The Darkness of Futile Thinking (Romans 1)

This progressive decay is not a novel invention of the modern age; it is the predictable and perennial consequence of humanity's decision to remove the Creator from the center of its existence. The Apostle Paul articulated this fatal flaw nearly two thousand years ago in his letter to the Romans, exposing the root of what I call the Progressively Vulgar:

> *For since the creation of the world God's invisible qualities—his eternal power and divine nature—have been clearly seen, being understood from what has been*

> *made, so that people are without excuse. For although they knew God, they neither glorified him as God nor thanked him, but their thinking became futile and their foolish hearts were darkened. Although they claimed to be wise, they became fools.*
>
> —Romans 1:20–22 NIV

This is the divine diagnosis of the modern condition. Their "*foolish hearts were darkened*" precisely because they refused to glorify Him as God or thank Him. Instead of building upon the foundation of eternal truth, they replace it with the flawed, shifting sands of human reason and societal construct, claiming to be wise while becoming fools. This descent is not only intellectual but spiritual, leading to the self-fulfilling prophecy detailed later in Romans 1: God gives them over to the very desires that are fueling their destructive trajectory.

Denying the Creator's Design

It is no wonder that we find ourselves in an age when our very identity is questioned. The world uses science in attempts to disprove the Bible, but they often hypocritically turn away from science and biology when it becomes inconvenient to their own versions of truth and reality.

Consider this example from the 2023 Bristol University Press article titled, "Analysing the 'Follow the Science' Rhetoric of Government Responses to COVID-19" in which the authors recount the following facts of life in a world no longer held to scientific standards or moral foundations:

> For much of 2020, as governments around the world scrambled to respond to the rapid rise in COVID-19 cases, political leaders in many high-income countries mobilized existing public health advisory systems, created new ones on the fly, and were bombarded with advice from scientists in universities and the private sector. What followed were repeated promises from political leaders that their decisions were based on the best available evidence and the advice from their science and public health advisors; in other words, that they were "following the science."[26]

This of course allowed world leaders to impose draconian rules upon the masses while turning our world upside down. They claimed to "follow the science," but if you dare to question their rules, you will be marginalized as a denier of absolute truth and tossed aside as ignorant and unworthy of any recognition for what you have to say.

---

[26] Margaret MacAulay, "Analysing the 'Follow the Science' Rhetoric of Government Responses to COVID-19," *Policy & Politics,* 51, no. 3 (2023); 466–485, https://doi.org/10.1332/030557321X16831146677554.

Yet somehow these same progressively vulgar ideologues find a way to stand on the other side of their own arguments when it becomes inconvenient, telling us, in essence, to deny science regarding the biology of the human being. They constructed an elaborate subset of reasoning that requires either a total buy-in through a denial of fact, a subservient partnership of ignorance to advance a shared ideal, or a path of mental gymnastics to arrive at their pre-defined juxtaposition. When the Obama administration failed in their attempts to change the law as it related to the definitions of male and female, the liberal mob of elitists turned their tack toward a newly defined relational conclusion—sex and gender are not one and the same. Oh, what a tangled web we weave when practicing the art of general deception to forward an agenda.

They will tell you it is quite simple: You might be born with every defining biological trait that qualifies as male, but your mind might tell you a completely different story that defines you as something else entirely. For those keeping score, there were eighty-one forms of gender identification as of 2024, and that list continues to grow. A basic internet search revealed seven gender categories that use the word *gender* in their description: gender apathetic, gender neutral, gender fluid, gender non-conforming, gender questioning, gender variant, and gender queer. What are we doing to those people that find themselves caught in a legitimate state of mental confusion or outright mental crisis? Treating these individuals with compassionate care that goes to the truth of the matter is not allowed; that is characterized as conversion therapy and in many locations can be punished under the law.

To further the dangers of this progressive radicalism that leaves no room for debate or questioning are the physiological impacts in research and medical treatments for a variety of conditions ranging from heart disease to cancer therapy.

In an age defined by complex global challenges—from public health crises to environmental degradation—rational decision-making is more critical than ever. However, a dangerous trend has emerged; there is a growing willingness to substitute verifiable scientific evidence with political, social, or ideological conviction. When core scientific principles are dismissed in favor of an agenda, the consequences are rarely abstract; they can be measured in real-world failures, financial waste, and, most critically, human suffering. The result is a perilous divide between ideology and reality, threatening foundational fields like medicine where biological truth is paramount to safe and effective treatment.

The critical importance of adhering to biological reality is starkly highlighted in the medical field, as demonstrated by a recent peer-reviewed study. The *Journal of Physiology* published a peer-reviewed paper on August 17, 2023, titled "Sex-Related Differences in Biology – Ignore Them at Your Peril," which detailed many of the consequences that come with this gender fluid approach to the science of biology and medical treatment. The following excerpt demonstrates the dangers of ignoring science when putting agenda above all else:

> Sex influences normal cardiac physiology as well as the organ's response to pathophysiological conditions. Compared with men, women have higher resting heart rates, longer QT intervals, greater parasympathetic responsiveness, smaller heart masses and smaller cardiac outputs. Once affected by cardiac disease, women often do not respond to established treatments as well as their male counterparts. This is the case following myocardial infarctions, coronary interventions and coronary artery bypass surgery. Women have a higher incidence of atrioventricular nodal re-entrant tachycardias and their longer QT intervals put them at greater risk of developing torsade de pointes, congenital, and acquired long-QT syndromes.
>
> Understanding sex differences in cardiac mechanisms is crucial to making a more effective translation of initial findings to the clinic and developing personalized medical treatments.[27]

---

[27] Ken McLeod, "Sex-Related Differences in Biology – Ignore Them at Your Peril," *The Journal of Physiology* 601, no. 18 (2023): 3983–3984, https://doi.org/10.1113/jp285313.

Society currently faces a crisis of authority because truth is no longer treated as a foundational objective. When academic institutions and scientific bodies allow subjective social constructs to redefine reality, they trade indisputable facts for fluid, individual feelings. This shift represents a deliberate strategy: the replacement of verifiable truth with ideological narratives that justify deceit as a tool for "social progress." We see this clearly in the "us versus them" techniques borrowed from political science, where facts are filtered through *motivated cognition*, which is defined as a phenomenon where individuals and institutions process information to fit preexisting tribal beliefs rather than objective reality.

A stark example of this was documented in a Nature.com report on narratives and opinion polarization regarding the origins of COVID-19. The report examined how the "Lab-Leap" narrative (suggesting human error or misconduct) was pitted against the "Natural-Origin" narrative. This wasn't merely a scientific debate; it was a psychological battlefield where the shaping of public opinion indirectly influenced subsequent research and dictated the policy responses of governments and universities. By framing one narrative as "scientific" and the other as "fringe" before the data was even settled, institutions weaponized the "common good" to suppress inquiry, deepening political divides and proving that when science is tethered to a narrative, the truth becomes an early casualty.[28]

---

[28] Armenak Antinyan, Thomas Bassetti, Luca Corazzini, and Filippo Pavesi, "Narratives and Opinion Polarization: A Survey Experiment,"

The Cult of the Godless State: Socialism and Communism

Is there nowhere to turn in this world of confusion and lies? The Progressively Vulgar has a political cousin: the Cult of the One-World Order, manifest in the dangerous, deceptive ideologies of socialism and communism. The fundamental flaw in all these systems is the same spiritual error: They are godless forms of government that replace our Creator with man-made institutions.

Socialism, in its practical application, is the gateway to communism because both seek to concentrate power and authority away from the individual and the family, placing it entirely in the hands of the all-powerful state. Both require the total surrender of personal liberty to the collective, which is administered by the *progressive elite*—the same foolish men who have convinced themselves they are wise.

The socialist promise is security and equity; the communist reality is forced submission and oppression. Their initial guarantees of shared resources quickly devolve into God's benevolent rule being replaced with man's tyrannical control. "*The fool says in his heart, 'There is no God*'" (Psalm 14:1 NIV), and the political manifestation of that foolishness is the system that seeks to eliminate all divine, transcendent authority. If God is removed, then the government becomes

---

Scientific Reports 14, no. 1 (2024), 19732, doi: 10.1038/s41598-024-70012-6.

the new god, demanding total faith, worship, and obedience, often enforced with the same brutality experienced by those marginalized for questioning its decrees. The attempt to create a heaven on earth without God inevitably results in a man-made hell. Why does this matter? Consider the future one-world leader that is detailed in the Bible, the antichrist, and you can logically deduce where this is headed.

The Urgent Call

Some have chosen a tentative place of spiritual compromise, where they acknowledge the existence of God but remain unwilling to step out in faith and fully accept Jesus. This position is precarious because a time is coming when the door to reconciliation will be permanently closed. Following that closure, the world will be governed by falsehoods, controlled by the one described in Scripture as the father of lies. He will introduce his Antichrist with a message of deceptive hope, leading many astray. The ultimate consequence of rejecting God is a terrible, eternal separation to face the final wrath of the very One who created you. While this condemnation is not God's desire for you, persistent denial of Jesus may lead Him to ultimately deliver you over to the path you have chosen.

To Reject Christ Is to Forfeit Everything

Why not consider a better path forward—one that comes with immediate peace that surpasses human understanding.

Do you live in fear wondering what is happening and feeling isolated and lost? God offers the way out through a relationship with Jesus, the one who loved us so much He came into this world to take all sin upon Himself. Even though Jesus was without sin, He paid our sin debt in full so that we could be reconciled with God. That gift of redemption is available to you right now; all you have to do is repent and acknowledge Christ as the Son of God and invite Him into your heart.

Hope is not lost; it exists for anyone and everyone through Jesus. The prophet Isaiah proclaimed the coming of the Messiah and even foretold of the one that would come before Him, John the Baptist whom he described as, "*The voice of one crying in the wilderness: Prepare the way of the Lord, make straight in the desert a highway for our God*" (Isaiah 40:3). When John the Baptist was confronted by the Levites from Jerusalem asking, "Who are you?" He replied, "I am not the Christ" (John 1: 19-20 ESV). They continued to question him, and we read this wonderful reply in verses 22 through 27:

> *So they said to him, "Who are you? We need to give an answer to those who sent us. What do you say about yourself?" He said: "I am the voice of one crying out in the wilderness, 'Make straight the way of the Lord,' as the prophet Isaiah said." (Now they had been sent from the Pharisees.) They asked him, "Then why are you baptizing, if you are neither the Christ, nor Elijah, nor the*

Prophet?" John answered them, "I baptize with water, but among you stands one you do not know, even he who comes after me, the strap of whose sandal I am not worthy to untie."

This is the good news for everyone; Jesus is the Messiah whom John the Baptist glorified in his day. Would that all believers embraced the mission of our testimony, as one crying out in the wilderness, following the stunning humbleness demonstrated by John. Even when his own disciples questioned him about the arrival of the Messiah, John pointed them to Jesus and away from himself: "*He must increase, but I must decrease*" (John 3:30).

All believers have a calling upon to share this gospel just as John the Baptist did. Along with John the Apostle who was one of the twelve that followed Christ during his earthly ministry, we stand at the end of this age and call out the warning to anyone that has ears to hear. Make no mistake, these are the final days: All is on full display to be seen just as foretold in the Bible.

If you have not opened that door to Jesus, asking him into your heart, consider yourself warned, not by me, but by His very words: "*There is a judge for the one who rejects me and does not accept my words; the very words I have spoken will condemn them at the last day*" (John 12:48 NIV).

This message may be seen as direct, even harsh or uncaring, but the urgency of the hour demands we set aside religious appeasement and declare the unvarnished truth. The fact is this: All have sinned and fallen short of the glory of God. Every person is tainted by sin, possessing no ability to save themselves. Only Jesus can redeem us through His selfless sacrifice, made in our stead. To dilute or water down the path to redemption is to erase the need for repentance entirely. Tragically, the contemporary church, seeking survival or relevance in this anti-Christian age, often chooses the easier route of half-truths. The true victims of this heresy are the lost—those most desperately in need of a clear path to God. What is required now is the same courage demonstrated by Paul: "*For I am not ashamed of the gospel of Christ: for it is the power of God unto salvation to every one that believeth; to the Jew first, and also to the Greek*" (Romans 1:16).

God's love is there for you to receive if you are willing to take that first step of faith in Christ. Jesus proclaimed, "*I am the way, and the truth, and the life. No one comes to the Father except through me*" (John 14:6 NIV).

Twenty-Seven:

THE WAY, THE TRUTH, AND THE LIFE – THE FINAL DECLARATION

> *In a world defined by chaos, fear, and uncertainty, Christ offers a peace that is both immediate and eternal.*

The human heart is hardwired for eternity. We relentlessly search for certainty, a destination, and an ultimate reality that gives meaning to the fleeting nature of our earthly lives. Before His crucifixion, knowing the path of suffering He was about to walk, Jesus delivered one of the most comforting and foundational promises to His closest disciples, a promise that resonates across millennia to every person today:

> *Let not your heart be troubled: ye believe in God, believe also in me. In my Father's house are many mansions: if it were not so, I would have told you. I go to prepare a place for you. And if I go and prepare a place for you, I will come again, and receive you unto myself; that where I am, there ye may be also. And whither I go ye know, and the way ye know.*
>
> —John 14:1–4

Pause and ponder the depth of that promise. Jesus speaks of a purpose far beyond this earthly existence, of a prepared place, a settled and secure destiny. He assures them, "*Let not your heart be troubled.*" In a world defined by chaos, fear, and uncertainty, Christ offers a peace that is both immediate and eternal. The solution to a troubled heart is faith—faith in God, and faith in Jesus.

The Pathway Revealed

Despite this profound assurance, the human tendency is to seek concrete directions, to ask for a map. Even Thomas, one of the twelve who had walked with Christ and witnessed firsthand His miracles and teachings, struggled to understand the meaning of His purpose. Thus, Thomas asked the ultimate question, which led to the greatest declaration for all mankind:

> *Thomas saith unto him, Lord, we know not whither thou goest; and how can we know the way? Jesus saith unto him, I am the way, the truth, and the life: no man cometh unto the Father, but by me.*
>
> —John 14:5–6

Jesus's statement is the cornerstone of Christian belief. It is the clearest possible declaration of Christ's exclusive identity and the solitary path to reconciliation with God. I am the way, the truth, and the life. No ambiguous routes, no multiple paths up the same mountain—only one way, one truth, and one life.

What Is Salvation?

What does it mean to be saved? How is a person saved? What is salvation? These terms are very common in the church family, but to the outsider or anyone not familiar with God's Word, they may be confusing. Another term many may have heard, to be "born again." Simply put, salvation means that our heavenly Father loved us so much that He gave us His only begotten Son as a sacrifice for everyone. To understand more about salvation, the best place to start is with one of the most familiar verses from the Bible: "*For*

God so loved the world, that he gave his only begotten son, that whosoever believes in him should not perish but have eternal life" (John 3:16). God's love for us is so strong that while we were shackled in sin, He gave us the perfect plan for salvation through Jesus. Romans 5:8 says: "*But God shows his love for us in that while we were still sinners, Christ died for us*" (ESV).

Why We Need Jesus

But faced with the urgency of this message, a common and perhaps deeply felt question emerges: Why do I need to do anything at all? Perhaps you believe you have lived a decent life; you follow the laws, uphold community standards, and make every effort not to steal or harm others. What is the point of salvation if I am already a "good" person? The error in this line of thinking is profound, for it confuses human merit with divine holiness. This line of reasoning does not take in account the reality of our condition: We are all sinners, universally falling short of God's perfect standard. God created us out of a foundational love, desiring an unbroken, intimate relationship with His creation. However, our sin, no matter how minor it seems by earthly metrics, creates an impassable gulf—a separation from His absolute holiness. While there are countless "good" people on this earth, we can never earn our way to salvation; we can never be "good enough" to find favor in God's perfect eyes. Our only remedy, our single path to the wonderful grace extended by God, is through the unmerited sacrifice of Jesus Christ, who gave His life as the sole payment for every person's debt.

> *The righteousness of God is through faith in Jesus Christ to all who believe, since there is no distinction. For all have sinned and fall short of the glory of God; they are justified freely by his grace through the redemption that is in Christ Jesus.*
>
> —Romans 3:22–24 CSB

The Free Gift and the Final Door

Do not allow the skepticism of this world to distract you from the truth revealed in Scripture. The consequence of rejecting God's moral standard is severe, as the Apostle Paul clearly states in Romans 6:23: "*For the wages of sin is death; but the free gift of God is eternal life in Christ Jesus our Lord*" (CSB). Mercifully, God provided the solution to this fatal debt through Jesus Christ. In perfect obedience to His Father's plan, Jesus took our sin upon Himself, dying on the cross and shedding His blood to make atonement for all humanity. On the third day, God demonstrated His ultimate victory by raising Jesus from the dead; He is now seated at the right hand of the Father.

Earlier in my life, I felt that same internal urgency, that quiet knock at the door of my heart, and I realized I was a sinner, spiritually lost in this world. One day, I took that step of faith and answered His call. If you have not yet made that profession of faith, you may be experiencing that same stirring within you. I can tell you beyond any doubt, that urging is the Holy Spirit of God speaking directly to your heart. We are all eternal spiritual beings who will live beyond this physical life, and we will one day stand before our Creator. Only by accepting the gift of salvation offered through Christ will we be acknowledged and welcomed into eternity.

We must take Christ at His word when He delivered the most challenging and sobering warning of His ministry. He was unequivocally clear that the path leading to life is not easy; rather, it is described as difficult, and the gate is narrow. The terrifying reality is that Christ Himself warns us that few will find it. We can spend our entire lives convincing ourselves that everything is okay, that our efforts are enough, or that we are inherently "right" with God simply because we are religious or "decent." Yet this self-assurance is a dangerous deception. If we have not first humbled ourselves before our Creator, openly confessed that we are sinners in need of rescue, and acknowledged by saving faith that Jesus died on the cross and was resurrected on the third day, our comfortable assumptions will mean nothing. Tragically, we could find ourselves standing before Him at the final judgment, anticipating reward, only to hear the most chilling and definitive of all proclamations: "*I never knew you: depart from me.*" The narrow path demands nothing less than the surrender of our pride and the acceptance of

His perfect, substitutionary grace because our destiny is not determined by our works, but by our personal knowledge and relationship with the Savior.

Twenty-Eight:

THE UPWARD CALL: NAVIGATING PAST, PRESENT, AND FUTURE

To move forward, we must shift our perspective and see ourselves through God's eyes—not as a collection of past mistakes but as beings created Imago Dei (in His image) and loved unconditionally.

Looking Back: Beyond Nostalgia and Regret

We often view the "good old days" through a filtered lens. While reminiscing brings comfort, there is a subtle danger in losing the context of days gone by. When we strip away the struggles of the past to remember only the simple things, we risk longing for a time that wasn't as perfect as we remember. This can rob us of our present hope, causing us to lose our footing in the here and now.

However, there is a more painful way we revisit the past: the "what-if" trap. We often wish we could revisit key moments to fix a mistake or make a different choice, thinking it would lead to greater success or self-worth. This cycle of regret is spiritually exhausting; it suggests that our mistakes are bigger than God's grace.

Moving Forward: From Paralysis to Purpose

The Bible offers a firm but loving correction for those stuck in the shadows of their past. We see a stark physical manifestation of this in Genesis 19:26, where Lot's wife was transformed into a pillar of salt. Her tragedy wasn't just a matter of turning her head; it was a heart-level paralysis. She was emotionally anchored to what she was leaving behind, rendering her unable to step into the deliverance God had provided.

Jesus echoed the necessity for forward momentum in Luke 9:62, warning that "*no one who puts a hand to the plow and looks back is fit for service in the kingdom of God*" (CSB). This isn't a demand for perfection, but a call for focus. To plow effectively, one must look toward the horizon; looking back causes the rows to become crooked and the work to stall. When we accept our past—scars and all—we allow God to:

- **Redeem the Failure:** He takes the things we are ashamed of and uses them to build empathy and wisdom.
- **Strengthen the Spirit:** Just as a muscle must be strained to grow, our faith is often fortified in the moments we feel most broken.
- **Prepare for Purpose:** By applying what we've learned through our mistakes, we become equipped for greater responsibilities. God doesn't waste a single tear or a single "wrong turn" if we are willing to hand the map back to Him.

Instead of wishing for a different past, let us embrace the one we have, knowing that God is the Master Architect. He is not looking for the version of you that never failed; He is calling the version of you that has been refined by fire and made ready to walk into the "new thing" He has prepared.

Seeing Ourselves Through the Divine Lens

To move forward, we must shift our perspective and see ourselves through God's eyes—not as a collection of past mistakes, but as beings created Imago Dei (in His image) and loved unconditionally. As James 1:2–4 reminds us, we are encouraged to "*consider it pure joy*" when we face trials, because the testing of our faith produces perseverance. This perseverance must finish its work so that we may be "*mature and complete.*"

God does not merely tolerate our history; He redeems it. He uses our scars to qualify us for greater responsibilities in His plan, turning our past "tests" into a future "testimony." Your history is not a weight to carry, but the training ground for where He is leading you next.

The Present: Contentment in a Modern Wilderness

Living in the "now" is not merely a psychological trick; it is a spiritual discipline. While the enemy uses the past to breed shame and the future to breed anxiety, God meets us exclusively in the current moment. He does not identify Himself as "I Was" or "I Will Be," but as "I am." To be present is to be where God is. However, in our modern era, the "now" has become a contested territory.

Living in the present has never been more difficult. We have become tethered to devices, driven by a pressing need to document every second rather than inhabit it. This "selfie culture" invites a subtle but dangerous shift: We stop experiencing our lives and start curating them. When the satisfaction of a moment is replaced by the dopamine hit of "likes," we drift toward the very pride that led to the fall of our greatest enemy—the desire to put ourselves at the center of the frame.

The Nature of Pride – The Paradox of Beauty

Lucifer was the angel of light, the most beautiful of God's created angelic hosts until pride took hold. It grew and festered until love of self, mixed with pride and envy, transformed this guardian of hosts into a beast filled with every evil desire. Consequently, he was cast out of God's presence. Lucifer's internal decay marked the first great irony of existence: that the very light that he was designed to carry became the fire that consumed his humility. As his fixation shifted from the Creator to the reflection of his own brilliance, the harmony of the heavens was fractured by a discordant ambition. No longer content to serve at the foot of the throne, he sought to ascend above it, trading his celestial inheritance for a kingdom of shadows. When his rebellion finally shattered against the firmament, he fell not just from a physical height, but from the height of grace itself, proving that even the most radiant spirit can be extinguished when it chooses its own glory over the source of all light.

We must ask ourselves: Can we truly enjoy the sunset if we are only viewing it through a lens to see how it will look on a social media feed? When we prioritize the display of our lives over the depth of our lives, we sacrifice the holy "now" on the altar of public vanity. This self-focus inevitably manifests as a lack of contentment. While it is godly to seek improvement—to pursue education, master a craft, or provide for our families—we must guard against the "covetous heart." God's moral boundaries were never meant to restrict our joy; they were designed to protect our peace.

If we enter the race of comparing our "behind-the-scenes" with everyone else's "highlight reel," we enter a race we can never win. The distraction of wants versus needs leads us back to a place of total self-absorption.

- **The Cycle of Never Enough:** When we believe happiness is one purchase or one "like" away, we become resentful toward our current circumstances, our loved ones, and eventually toward God Himself.
- **The Manna Principle:** Just as the Israelites could not store manna for the next day, we cannot store up contentment from yesterday's achievements. It must be found fresh today in the sufficiency of Christ.

The Renewal of the Mind

True peace is not found in the acquisition of more things, bigger homes, or newer automobiles. Those are fleeting shadows that cannot fill a soul made for eternity. Our worth is not a fluctuating currency based on our status or our "reach."

Why limit ourselves by defining our self-worth in what this world offers, the shallow existence of possessions and status, when we can free our hearts and minds through a focus on the eternal. God provides a life of purpose, fulfillment, and meaning that transcends the empty pursuits of this brief time on earth. This shift in perspective acts as an anchor in a world of shifting sands. While material achievements are subject to the erosion of time and the fickleness of public opinion, an identity rooted in the divine is immutable. When we anchor our value in the eternal, we are no longer exhausted by the relentless "treadmill of more," where every milestone only reveals another mountain to climb. Instead, we find a profound stillness in knowing we are already known and loved. That realization transforms our labor from a desperate grab for validation into a joyful expression of service, turning our brief earthly stay into a meaningful prelude to something far greater.

As Romans 12:2 instructs, we find transformation through the renewal of our minds. This renewal allows us to see that the present moment—no matter how quiet or unglamorous—is enough because God is in it. When we stop trying to "frame" our lives for the world, we finally become free to live them for Him. We move from being performers for a digital audience to being stewards of a divine gift: the gift of today.

Turning Presence into Purpose

Making the most of the "now" requires a shift in our spiritual posture. It is about being fully engaged with the people, tasks, and divine appointments right in front of us.

- **The "Present" as a Gift:** The present is the only space where we can exercise faith, offer love, and make choices. We cannot serve our neighbor in the past, and we cannot worship God in the future. We must walk daily in our faith.

- **Cultivating Awareness:** Expansion of the soul happens when we stop waiting for "the next big thing" and start looking for God in the "small things." Whether it is a conversation with a friend or a quiet moment of reflection, these are the building blocks of a life well-lived.

Leaving the past behind is an act of trust. It is a declaration that you believe God's plan for your future is greater than your history. You are not a finished product; you are a work in progress, and the "now" is the canvas upon which God is currently painting. As Philippians 3:13–14 beautifully captures, we should be "*forgetting what is behind and straining toward what is ahead*" (NIV) as we press on toward the prize.

The Future: Purposeful Vision Instead of Anxious Control

The past is part of God's architectural plan, and the present is His gift of a life redeemed; the future is a God-given stewardship. Many of us approach the horizon with a spirit of anxiety, attempting to prognosticate our way into security. But as we have learned through the renewal of our minds, the future is not a place of fear, but the destination of God's unfolding plan.

Spiritual self-discipline helps us stay grounded in trust, knowing that God has a plan and purpose for our lives, and through this we have peace that surpasses our ability to understand. The path that lies beyond the horizon is prepared by our loving heavenly Father with our needs met before we even know to seek His help. Accepting this discipline is not a burden of rules, but a rhythmic "re-tuning" of the soul to a frequency higher than our immediate anxieties. It is the daily practice of surrendering our need for control at the feet of One who sees the beginning from the end. By making space for prayer, reflection, and stillness, we cultivate a "proactive peace," a spiritual reservoir that remains full even when the world around us feels depleted. This foresight of the Divine ensures that as we step into the unknown of tomorrow, we are not walking into a void, but into a landscape already meticulously provisioned by God's grace. Contentment in the now allows us to look at the future and say, "I do not know what the years hold, but I know Who holds the years."

Our history—the very "pillars of salt" and "crooked plow lines" we've moved past—serves a purpose here. God does not waste the trials of our past; He converts them into the wisdom required for our future. As we move forward, we carry the "perseverance" described in James 1.

This is the bridge: The testing of yesterday becomes the testimony of tomorrow. We are being prepared for "greater responsibilities in His plan." This isn't just about personal success; it's about being fit for His kingdom. When we stop looking back and stop comparing our "now" with the circumstances of others, we will finally be light enough to run the race set before us.

By leaving the past to God's mercy, the present to His grace, and the future to His providence, we find a life of wholeness. We no longer need to be the center of the frame because we are part of a much larger, more beautiful picture. We move forward not because we have all the answers, but because we are following the One who is the Alpha and the Omega—the beginning and the end.

The Upward Call

With each new day we are stepping into a fresh territory of grace. This transition offers us a holy pause—a moment to survey the horizon and ensure our compass is still pointed toward True North. To make the most of every opportunity, we must be willing to engage in the brave work of self-examination.

Our resolution should be a "holy reversal" that guides us away from our own basic earthly desires toward a focused discipline that seeks to lift up those around us. We must strive to be like Christ, the one who existed entirely for the Father and for others. We move from the "selfie," a life framed by self-interest, to the "neighbor," a life expanded by selfless love.

Anchored in Grace, Guided by Truth

Remember the foundational truth of the gospel: God loved us before we ever turned a thought toward Him. He sent

His Son as the ultimate sacrifice for our transgressions, not just to forgive our past, but to liberate our future. Because of the cross, we are not required to dwell in the suffocating shame of our mistakes. Instead, we are invited to walk in the "newness of life."

To live a life of impact, we must adopt the discipline of the "fixed gaze." As Proverbs 4:25 suggests: "*Let your eyes look straight ahead; fix your gaze directly before you*" (NIV). When we stop looking back at what paralyzed us and stop looking sideways at what others are doing, we can finally begin to build. We are not just building careers or reputations; we are building a life that reflects His kingdom. Every act of kindness, every moment of integrity, and every step of faith is a brick in the architecture of the world for which we ultimately long: Heaven.

Twenty-Nine:

SIMPLY CHRIST: THE SUMMATION AND THE SINGULAR FOCUS

"The grass withereth, the flower fadeth: but the word of our God shall stand forever."

—Isaiah 40:8

Throughout *Beyond the Broad Path*, we have charted the society's descent into what I termed the Progressively Vulgar, a culture marked by the arrogant marginalization of anyone who adheres to objective truth. We exposed the foolishness described in Romans 1:21–22, showing that human thinking has become futile, leading to the hypocrisy of claiming to "follow the science" when it supports an agenda but conveniently denying fundamental biology when it challenges manufactured social constructs. We saw how this spiritual error finds its political expression in socialism and communism, godless forms of government that replace the Creator's authority with man-made institutions and seek to establish a cult of the one-world order. I believe that this is the path that Jesus referred to as the broad road that leads to destruction.

As we noted, "religion" is not the answer either. In fact I assert that religion has been corrupted to fit specific narratives and agendas; it has moved so far from the truth that one could easily conclude that religion has failed. Many congregations and denominations have lost the primary objective of Christianity and fallen away from the foundation of God's Word, which remains true: "*The grass withereth, the flower fadeth: but the word of our God shall stand forever*" (Isaiah 40:8).

The Problem of Human Effort and Religion

Religion is defined as a system of beliefs, practices, and attitudes that relate to the sacred or the divine. By some measures, there are 10,000 religions or denominations across the world. But there is only one Christ, the only one who made a substitutional sacrifice of love, laying down His life on the cross to pay for all our sins. Religions take on many shapes and forms with most acknowledging our struggle with imperfections. Some seek wisdom and fulfillment through the mind and body; these paths point toward a goal of perfection, claiming that meditation and mind control will lead one to a place of higher awareness.

Except for Christianity, all religions exclude the teaching that Jesus is the way, the truth, and the life. Although some religions include references to the name of Jesus, they deny His deity and power. Sadly, faith and deception often intertwine in the form of a transactional affiliation—a spiritual *quid pro quo* that subtly denies the sufficiency of Christ. This manifests in many ways, from the self-help gurus of the East to the modern television evangelists who mask schemes of personal profit behind a veil of promised returns. In those circles, the "prosperity" or "word of faith" narrative reduces our relationship with the Creator to a bargain. It is a troubling sight: false religious figures adding wealth and power to their own lives through schemes and deception while the downtrodden are encouraged to "sow" money they cannot afford to give in hopes of a brighter day. This framework suggests God can be moved by our formulas, obscuring the truth that His grace is a sovereign gift, not a product of our leverage.

Other deceptions seek to rebuild the barriers that Christ already tore down. Some institutions require worshipers to navigate a man-made hierarchy, confessing transgressions to men and performing assigned penance to earn favor from above. Still others claim a "completed" version of God's Word, doled out through secret revelations given to a single individual. This often results in a spiritual Ponzi scheme, where the living are tasked with performing good deeds or rituals to secure the standing of those who have already passed.

Whether the practice is a throwback to the observance of old festivals and feasts as a requirement for holiness or the pantheistic blurring of the Creator with His creation, these deviations share a common flaw. They replace the finished work of the cross with a checklist of human efforts. By requiring their followers to earn or bargain for what has already been bought at a price, these false gospels ultimately offer a shadow in place of the Light.

The Apostle Paul offers this succinct definition of life as a believer in Christ, which removes all these distractions through a clarifying narrative of God's enduring grace:

> *I have been crucified with Christ and I no longer live, but Christ lives in me. The life I now live in the body, I live by faith in the Son of God, who loved me and gave himself for me. I do not set aside the grace of God, for if righteousness could be gained through the law, Christ died for nothing.*
>
> —Galatians 2:20–21 CSB

The Bedrock of Salvation

Paul directly asserts the bedrock upon which all Christianity must stand: the cross is the foundation upon which salvation rests. This truth eliminates every other human effort or requirement. Ponder that for a moment, and then consider the most poignant example from the book of Luke as Jesus and the repentant thief are being crucified. In his final, agonizing moments, the thief expressed a simple faith that bypassed all earthly ritual:

> *We are punished justly, for we are getting what our deeds deserve. But this man has done nothing wrong. Then he said, "Jesus, remember me when you come into your kingdom." Jesus answered him, "Truly I tell you, today you will be with me in paradise."*
>
> —Luke 23:41–43 NIV

In those final minutes of life, did the thief have time to pay penance? To join a denomination? To perform years of good works? Absolutely not. His desperate plea was answered with the ultimate promise of immediate grace. This demonstrates unequivocally that salvation is found only through Jesus Christ and His resurrection. The moment we attempt to supplement the cross with anything else—any ritual, any deed, any level of personal goodness—we nullify the entire act. As Paul so rightly declares, to add anything to Christ's finished work is to say that Christ died for nothing. The cross is all-sufficient; it is everything.

Simply Christ

We have established that the wages of sin is death, and that all have sinned and fall short of the glory of God. We have established that only Jesus is the way, the truth, and the life. Where do you stand with God? Are you weary and tired of this world? Does it feel like everything is piling up, weighing you down? Do you feel like nobody cares?

God cares

Listen to these words and take notice: God loves you! You were loved by God before you were formed in the womb. God loves you so much that He sent Jesus to live among us, to experience what we face, the hardships, temptations, disappointments of this world. And in total obedience to God, Jesus laid down His life for you. Your debt of sin is paid in full, and all you have to do is believe in your heart and invite Christ into your life. The message is simple, and it represents the truth of the gospel, the good news, that all people can be saved—not a few based on status or race. The gospel of Jesus Christ is a message of hope for everyone. Christ alone is the antidote to the Progressively Vulgar spirit of our age.

What does it mean to be a follower of Christ, not religion? It means embracing a new identity:

- **We are Created in God's Image:** We are all created by God, in His own image. No political agenda or social construct can ever usurp this fundamental, divine identity. Do you truly believe in the intrinsic value God placed on you when He formed you?

- **We Are One Family:** Through our shared faith in Jesus, we are one family, united not by human rules, but by the Holy Spirit.
- **We Share a Transcendent Peace:** We share a peace that surpasses all understanding (Philippians 4:7), a rest promised by Jesus: "*Come to me, all you who are weary and burdened, and I will give you rest*" (Matthew 11:28 NIV). Are you ready to lay down your burden of self-effort and receive this rest?
- **We Live in Forgiveness:** We are forgiven just as we strive to forgive others (Colossians 3:13). The transactional nature of religion is replaced by the complete grace of the cross.
- **We Embrace Service:** We put Christ first in all things and embrace His servant attitude, placing others and their needs above our own (Philippians 2:3–5). This is the true meaning of Christian inclusion—not political tolerance, but sacrificial love.
- **We Shine the Light:** We will all continue to strive to live out our faith, sharing it with gentleness and respect to others (1 Peter 3:15), shining

> the light of Jesus and His love throughout this dark and lost world. I say we put away religion and share Christ instead. Simply Christ.

The message of *Beyond the Broad Path* serves as a warning, a declaration, and an invitation. The warning is clear: Denying foundational truth, whether in science or salvation, carries severe consequences. Our declaration stands firm: Jesus Christ is the only way, the only truth, and the only life. Now, the ball is firmly in your court. If you have not yet laid down your heavy burdens and accepted God's gift of salvation, ask yourself: What is preventing me from saying yes to the One who offers eternal peace?

If you have accepted Christ, the invitation to a new life now becomes a vital challenge. Are you living for Christ with a vibrant testimony that shines through your actions and your words? If your answer is **yes**, then stay the course with diligence, trusting in the guidance of the Holy Spirit and keeping to the path of God's will for your life. If the answer is no, do not waste another moment living in guilt or dwelling on past failures. Seize this moment to step up and step out in renewed faith. Strive to run the spiritual race before you and finish strong, enduring to the end to the glory of God.

May His grace and peace be your constant companions as you continue beyond the broad path.

Conclusion:

FINDING THE PATH

The Echoes of a Fallen World (Recapping the Chaos)

We have navigated the treacherous currents of the modern world together, examining the chaos that threatens to engulf us. Look around and listen: We hear the rumblings of wars and rumors of wars. We witness an accelerating spirit of lawlessness. We see self-interest elevated and applauded as virtue; it is a doctrine taught from platforms of influence: "Self above all else."

But the gospel of self stands in radical, irreconcilable opposition to the truth that anchors the true gospel, which is the call of Jesus Christ to deny self and place the needs of others first. We have arrived at the precipice where these two realities clash.

The Truth Revealed: From Prophecy to Person

Our journey has been grounded in the immovable truth of Scripture. Old Testament prophets, speaking across millennia of shadows, pointed toward the coming light: the Messiah. The New Testament does not merely speculate; it reveals His arrival in the person of Jesus of Nazareth, fully man and fully God, the Incarnation of love and sacrifice.

His supreme act was the ultimate denial of self. When He said, "This is my body," He wasn't merely offering a symbol; He was giving the substance, His life, to pay the debt of sin that we, trapped in the cycle of self, could never hope to pay. This is the cornerstone of our faith.

The Two Voices: Choice and Sacrifice

We live in an age where the rhetoric of autonomy reigns supreme. We hear the mantra of the new age: "My body, my choice," used to justify the termination of life within the womb. Yet, the womb, which was the very means of our Savior's entry into the world, offers the most profound rebuttal. Jesus could have simply appeared—descended in glory—but God's divine plan was the miracle of the virgin birth, beginning in the most vulnerable human space, the womb, to reveal His only begotten Son. This act declares that life is sacred from its very inception and that the ultimate choice was made by the Son of God who chose to give Himself up, that "*whoever believes in him will not perish, but have everlasting life*" (John 3:16).

The Narrow Way Demands Our All

And so, we stand at the threshold, facing the choice laid out in the Gospels—the broad path, which is easy and leads to destruction, or the narrow path, which is difficult and found by few. Every moment of inaction, every hesitation at this crossroads, is a choice, a passive agreement to remain on the broad, comfortable, and ultimately destructive path, thereby denying the active calling of God.

The narrow way is not passive belief; it is fierce discipleship. It demands a daily, active commitment to deny ourselves and to pick up our cross and follow Him. The question is existential: Are we, the called, truly living out the rigorous, self-denying mandate placed upon us as believers? If the light of Christ is not shining brightly from our lives in this darkening world, then who will illuminate the way?

Final Summation: The Time is Now

With our journey through *Beyond the Broad Path* complete, you have reached a point of decision for your journey forward:

- **To Skeptics and Seekers:** Will you retreat to the comfort of the broad path, or will you take the courageous first step of faith, surrendering your own way, to gain eternal life and join Christ on the narrow way?
- **To Believers:** If you have grown cold, if you have become distracted by the world's trappings, or if you have simply grown weary and lost your enthusiasm for Christ, today is the moment of your re-commissioning. Stand up! Are you ready to leave the baggage of doubt, self-loathing, bitterness, and unresolved anger behind you?

The time for contemplation is over. The time for decision is here. The crossroads are set, the paths are clear, and the calling is unmistakable. The narrow way awaits. Will you take it?

The Prayer of Acceptance

Dear Heavenly Father,

I have been searching to fill a void in my life, and today I finally understand that the only way to fulfillment is through Jesus Christ. I believe that Jesus is the true Son of God, that He came to this earth, lived a perfect life, and gave His life as the ultimate sacrifice for my sins. I believe that Jesus died on the cross and was resurrected to life on the third day, defeating both sin and death, and paying my debt so that I can receive the gift of eternal life. I confess that I am a sinner, and today, I sincerely accept Jesus as my personal Savior, and I ask Him to come into my heart. Thank you, Lord, for the gift of salvation, the forgiveness of my sins, and the promise of new life.

Amen.

ACKNOWLEDGEMENTS

My deepest gratitude belongs first and foremost to my wife for her enduring love, patience, and support over four decades. Our life together is the ultimate testimony as we strive to put Christ first in all things. To my eldest daughter, whose tremendous faith and motivation shine as a joyous light – thank you.

To the readers and ministry partners of Life Beyond Horizons Ministry, your engagement with the theological essays and your commitment to sharing the Gospel message have been the true inspiration for the pages of this book.

Finally, I am deeply grateful to my publisher for believing in this message and providing the platform and support in my quest to help readers find peace and spiritual fulfillment.

www.ingramcontent.com/pod-product-compliance
Lightning Source LLC
LaVergne TN
LVHW010605100826
845148LV00014B/2852

* 9 7 8 1 6 3 2 9 6 9 9 2 7 *